THE WONDERFUL WORLD OF NATURE

Edited by

MAURICE BURTON

Illustrated by

PETER BARRETT

OCTOPUS

Contents

First published in 1979 by
Octopus Books Limited
59 Grosvenor Street
London W1

© 1978 Flammarion
This edition © 1979 Octopus Books Limited
Original French text by Michel Cuisin
Translated by Elizabeth Cooper

ISBN 0 7064 1087 4

Printed in Italy by A. Mondadori, Verona

The World of Nature

Where does our Earth come from? How was it formed? Scientists still have not come up with the final answers to these questions. They have certainly put forward theories on the subject, but these have not yet been proved conclusively. In just the same way, we still know very little about the origin of living beings and the very nature of life.

The living cell, which is the building block of all animals and plants, has been the subject of much study. We now know many of its secrets. And yet, nobody has ever succeeded in making a complete cell. Nor have they been able to give it life.

In the course of the Earth's history more and more sophisticated species have developed, but no one knows how it has happened. However, during the nineteenth century scientists put forward the theory of evolution – that the different groups of living beings were descended one from the other, the animals following one evolutionary path and the plants another.

The first living beings are thought to have been micro-organisms, minute creatures visible only under a microscope. They evolved gradually over millions of years and gave rise to molluscs (such as snails and mussels for example) on the one hand and to crustaceans (such as crabs and lobsters) on the other. Likewise, mammals and birds are descended from certain reptiles.

Many people found the theory of evolution difficult to accept, but there are several facts which at least partly confirm it. Men have studied fossils, the remains of animals and plants which lived millions of years ago, and have shown that only the very simplest creatures are to be found in the most ancient rocks. The oldest animal fossils date back little more than 600 million years, and the first plants, even simpler than the algae, lived 2,500 million years ago.

Recent studies of sedimentary deposits have uncovered fish in rocks as old as 450 million years, as well as amphibians (animals that live partly in water and partly on land) which no longer exist.

The first reptiles were found in rocks formed 300 million years ago. We know that the dinosaurs lived for 165 million years before becoming extinct 70 million years ago.

Unfortunately, we do not know the total number of animal and plant species that became extinct in the course of this evolutionary process, because many of them did not leave any fossil remains, especially those which had no hard parts in their bodies. Likewise, we still do not know the total number of species living today. However, more than 371,000 species of plants and nearly 1,200,000 species of animals have already been counted, and it is estimated that there would have been nearly 500,000 plant species and several million animal species.

A species is made up of a number of animals or plants that are able to reproduce amongst themselves, and whose offspring can go on doing the same indefinitely. The plant kingdom comprises flowering plants (about 227,000 species) and non-flowering plants (12,000 ferns, 26,000 mosses, more than 33,000 seaweeds, 50,000 mushrooms, about 20,000 lichens, 1,600 bacteria and 2,000 blue-green algae).

In the animal kingdom man has counted 880,000 living species of insects (although according to some specialists in the field there could be four or five million), 127,000 species of molluscs, 25,000 species of crustaceans, 57,000 species of spiders and related animals, 38,000 species of worms, 28,000 species of protozoa (animals consisting of only one cell), 10,000 myriapods (a creature with a thousand feet), 4,800 sponges, 5,300 coelenterates (sea-anemones and corals), 6,000 echinoderms (sea-urchins, starfishes) – most of them without an internal skeleton and none having a skeleton of bone.

On the other hand, there are only 42,000 living species of vertebrates (animals with backbones). Of these there are 50 species without jaws (lampreys), 550 species of cartilaginous fishes (rays and sharks), 20,000 species of bony fishes (carp, tunny fish and others), 2,500 species of amphibians (frogs, salamanders), 6,100 species of reptiles (snakes, lizards, crocodiles, tortoises), 8,600 species of birds and 4,200 species of mammals.

Man himself is part of the animal kingdom. He is a mammal. He differs from other mammals in several ways. He has the use of language, he is able to imagine and to think, and he is more intelligent than any other species. He has had and continues to have a very great effect on nature, but he depends entirely upon the natural world and cannot live without it. He needs plants, for they supply him with food and produce the oxygen which he breathes. It is absolutely vital that he should have knowledge of the natural world in order to have a better understanding and appreciation of it. He must learn to respect and use wisely the resources which are available to him.

For nature is not just a collection of plants and animals. It is also the air, the water and the earth. It is the medium in which all organisms live.

For our study of nature, we have deliberately chosen only a very small number of living creatures. Peter Barrett's illustrations show the beauty and diversity of the plants and animals described in the text.

Name of the period	Main Subdivisions	
Azoic		
Proterozoic or Crytozoic	Precambrian	
Paleozoic (Primary Era)	Cambrian	
	Silurian	
	Devonian	
	Carboniferous	
	Permian	
Mesozoic (Secondary Era)	Triassic	
	Jurassic	
	Cretaceous	
Cenozoic (Tertiary and Quaternary Eras)	Tertiary	
	Quaternary	

Historical Table of Plants and Animals

Beginning (in millions of years before our age)	Animal and Plant Characteristics
4,000	Neither animal nor vegetable life.
2,500	700 million years ago, the first indications of the existence of seaweeds and invertebrates.
600	By now all the different types of invertebrates are present, as well as seaweeds. All live in the sea. The dominant animals are trilobites.
425	The first plants and animals on land, the animals including scorpions and myriapods, and primitive fishes.
405	The first amphibians (land vertebrates), also spiders and ammonites, tree ferns and lycopods. In the sea, corals.
345	Forests of ferns, rushes and giant lycopods, the first conifers and first reptiles.
280	First beetles appear. Numerous reptiles. Disappearance of trilobites.
230	Appearance of dinosaurs. Calcareous algae and conifers are the dominant plant life.
180	Appearance of the first birds (archaeopteryx) and the first mammals.
135	The first flowering plants. Gradual disappearance of the dinosaurs and the ammonites. First marsupials and first insect-eating mammals.
63	Giant land mammals. Giant birds. Amphibians and reptiles decrease in numbers. Numerous flowering plants.
3	Mammoths and sabre-toothed tiger. First appearance of man.

9

Prehistoric Life

The fossilized remains of the ancestors of modern-day animals have been found in quarries and cliffs. Most of these fossils are no more than impressions in the rock or single bones. From the fossils we know that the first living creatures were algae and invertebrates. Later there appeared animals and plants which had a much more complex structure. By examining the skeletal remains of these, scientists could put together a more or less accurate picture of them. In this way they were able to divide the history of the Earth into several major periods which were called eras. Each of these was characterized by different types of flora and fauna.

For example, let us look at the Secondary Era. Throughout this period there lived reptiles which were markedly different from those we see today. They were the dinosaurs, which included some of the largest land animals. Many

pteranodons

plesiosaurs

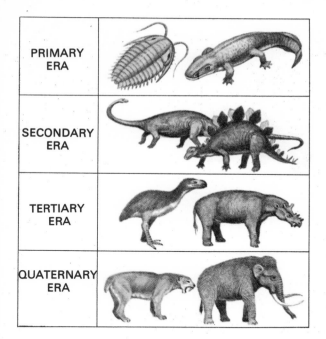

PRIMARY ERA	
SECONDARY ERA	
TERTIARY ERA	
QUATERNARY ERA	

were four-legged. Some of them lived in the sea and looked like fishes, while others resembled birds. They were completely different from the animals we are familiar with today.

Among the animals of the Secondary Era were fish-like reptiles, the ichthyosaurs. Their remains have been found in Europe, America and Greenland. They were shaped something like dolphins or sharks, for they had flippers, a fin on the back, a forked tail and long jaws lined with teeth. The largest were 10 m (33 ft) or more long, judging by the size of their teeth. It is thought that they fed on fish and molluscs.

There were other reptiles called plesiosaurs. They usually had very long necks. Having adapted to life in the sea, they swam near the surface some of the time, and caught fish, molluscs and small pterodactyls. Some of them

are thought to have come out on land where they wandered about as awkwardly as the present-day sea turtles. Like the turtle, the plesiosaur must have laid its eggs on land, thus risking its safety away from its native element.

The flying reptiles, known as pterosaurs or pterodactyls, lived at about the same time as the first birds, but they were not their direct ancestors. Among them were the largest flying animals that have ever lived – the pteranodons. Judging from the fossils of certain species discovered in North America, their wing span was 7.5 m (25 ft).

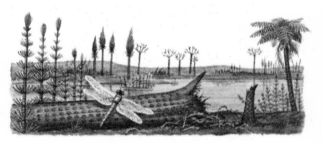

Reconstruction of landscape in the Carboniferous period. The giant dragonfly had a wingspan of up to 1 m (3 ft).

Woolly rhinoceros and two woolly mammoths of the Quaternary Era.

Reptiles of the Secondary Era in the sea, on land and in the air.

ichthyosaurs

The Seashore

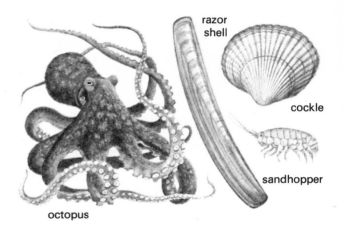

razor shell

cockle

sandhopper

octopus

Seashores everywhere are either rocky or sandy, broken up here and there with rocks or sandy beaches. Near the mouths of large rivers the shore may be little but mud.

All year round the sea rises and sinks back, usually twice every twenty-four hours. These movements of the sea are called the tides. There is little sign of tides on most of the shores of the Mediterranean, but elsewhere at low tide the waters recede, sometimes 2–3 km ($1\frac{1}{2}$–2 miles) where the beach slopes only slightly. The area between high and low tidemarks is known as the tidal zone, or littoral.

On the pieces of seaweed and other debris which has been thrown up by the sea tiny sand-hoppers can be found. These are almost transparent. They hop like fleas, but unlike true fleas, which are insects, they are crustaceans. When disturbed, they leap 20–30 cm (8–12 in). They feed on bits of seaweed, the bodies of dead seagulls or other animals and live on wet sand in which they like to bury themselves. The female carries up to seventeen eggs in a pouch. When these hatch, the larvae from them become part of plankton. They shed their outer covering several times as they grow. These little animals live for about a year and a half.

Sometimes the common hermit crab can be seen between the tidemarks with a sea-anemone attached to its shell. These two animals live in a symbiotic relationship (each depending on the other for its existence). The hermit crab is protected by its companion's tentacles, which have stinging cells, and the anemone has a handy means of transport from one feeding ground to another.

There are 1,600 species of starfishes in the world. These and sea-urchins, which are spiny and look a bit like hedgehogs, belong to the group of animals known as echinoderms (or spiny skins). The starfish lives on mussels, which it opens by separating the two hinged parts of the shell which are called valves.

lugworm

crab

12

top shell

shrimp

limpet

barnacles

The octopus, which may be up to 30 cm (12 in) long, excluding its eight tentacles, each of which has two rows of suckers, is not a dangerous creature. It lies in wait for its prey in a hole in a rock. When disturbed, it changes colour and sends out a cloud of black ink as a cover for its escape from its enemies.

At low tide there can be seen little whirls in the wet sand. These are the marks left by sea-worms called lugworms. These animals swallow sand, digesting anything edible in it, and discard the rest in the form of whirls on the surface. The lugworm never leaves its burrow, not even to reproduce.

There are many molluscs which bury themselves in the wet sand. They have tubes or siphons which they push up to the surface. One siphon takes in water, from which oxygen is extracted, and also plankton for food, while the other expels waste matter and the filtered water.

The rocks, exposed at low tide and covered at high tide, provide a habitat for thousands of little animals. The most numerous are the barnacles, which are like shellfish with their conical-shaped shell, open at the top. They live in colonies of thousands on the rocks, and also attach themselves to the shells of mussels, limpets and winkles. At low tide these crustaceans appear to be dead, but the plates of their shell retain enough air and moisture to protect them from the sun and wind. When covered by the sea, these plates open and six pairs of legs are pushed out to catch plankton. A barnacle can live for six years or more.

The edible mussel is another inhabitant of the rocks. Colonies of these live in the cracks of rocks or may cover the entire rock surface.

Periwinkles, or winkles for short, stand on their one foot. They are called sea-snails or gastropods and are related to limpets, which have striped, conical shells.

turnstone

mussels

sea-anemone

winkle

hermit crab

The Sandy Beach

At low tide sandy beaches look bare of life. There is hardly anything to be seen but empty shells and here and there pieces of seaweed or a cuttlebone or two. The empty shells will include razor shells, small shells known as tellins, which are sometimes lilac or yellow on the inside, and cockle shells, which have distinct growth-lines on the outside of the shell.

Animals and plants on rocky coasts are not the same as those on sandy beaches because their living conditions are entirely different. The chief difference lies in this, that on rocky shores are found plants and animals that must have a solid surface on which to fasten themselves. On rocky coasts, for example, there is much more seaweed and many more varieties than on sandy beaches. These plants, the body of which is called a thallus, have neither flowers, stem, leaves nor roots as we know them in flowering plants. A seaweed attaches itself to a rock or a pebble by what is called a holdfast. They reproduce by means of spores, which are microscopic cells contained in little chambers generally found at the end of the thallus. Seaweed can be seen at low tide on the exposed rocks, where it appears to grow like grass.

Sea-wracks are among the most common seaweeds. Some have floats on them which may be arranged in pairs. They and the oar-weeds belong to the brown seaweeds. Pieces of sea-wrack are constantly being torn off by the waves and thrown up on the beaches, where they gather to form heaps of kelp. The oar-weed looks like glossy, embossed straps or ribbons, sometimes reaching a length of 3–4 m (10–13 ft) and a width of 10–30 cm (4–12 in). Brown seaweeds can be found growing to a depth of 30 m (100 ft).

Green seaweed, the thallus of which contains chlorophyll, cannot survive unless it is close to the surface so that it can receive bright light.

marram grass

The deeper you go underwater, the darker it becomes, because water absorbs the light rays of the sun; at a depth of 500 m (1,650 ft) there is total darkness. One of the most common green seaweeds is the sea-lettuce. The thallus looks like a very delicate lettuce leaf, being bright green and rather crinkled around the edges.

Finally, there are the red seaweeds, which do not need as much light, and grow at depths of between 60 and 80 m (200–250 ft).

On some beaches it is possible to find two species of eel grass called zostera and posidonia. They look like seaweeds, but they are flowering plants – the only ones to live on the murky bottom of the sea.

Above the high tidemark there may be sand dunes, and in these there are often thick clumps of permanent vegetation. They are like miniature deserts, for the rain sinks into the sand very quickly, and the wind causes a shift in the sand and the sun dries out the surface. The plants which grow in this environment all have an in-

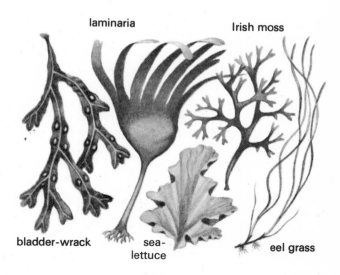

laminaria Irish moss

bladder-wrack sea-lettuce eel grass

built protection against the dryness. For example, the sea-rush has roots which go down a long way in search of water and form a dense network underground. This network holds the sand together, preventing it from shifting.

rock pipit

sea holly

convolvulus

15

The Rocky Shore

Seas and oceans cover nearly three-quarters of the surface of the Earth. It is in the polar seas that living creatures are most numerous. Conditions there are perfect for plankton, which attracts schools of fish and big colonies of birds. In comparison, life in tropical seas is concentrated around the coral reefs, teeming with many species of invertebrates and fishes.

sea otter

The biggest animal ever to have lived on the planet Earth is the blue whale or rorqual. It spends a large part of the year in cold seas, and the only time it goes near tropical seas is to breed. This species has been hunted so intensively that it is now protected to save it from extinction. The biggest blue whale on record was 33.27 m (110 ft) long and the heaviest weighed 190 tonnes. The blue whale is called a whalebone whale because its teeth have been replaced by baleen or whalebone.

dolphin

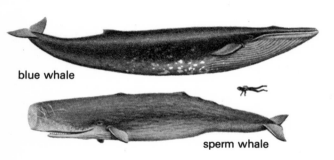

blue whale

sperm whale

Different from the blue whale is the cachelot or sperm whale. This whale has teeth and eats vast quantities of squid, which it pursues down to depths of 1,000 m (3,500 ft) or more.

The sea otter is another marine mammal which spends most of its life in the water. It lives close to rocky coasts and reefs in the northern Pacific Ocean, around the Commander, Kurile and Aleutian islands and off California. It is often seen lying on its back at the surface, eating shellfish, sea-urchins and crabs, for which it dives to a depth of 60 m (200 ft). The Californian sea otter uses a stone as an anvil on which to break open the outer covering of sea-urchins and shellfish.

The wandering albatross nests on the remote Antarctic islands such as South Georgia, Macquarie Islands and Kerguelen. It is estimated that there are 20,000 breeding pairs, as well as the non-breeding birds. In December this albatross lays a single egg which hatches out after 78 days incubation. The albatross chick stays in the nest for an average of 275 days and is fed by its parents. At one month it weighs 2,900 g (6 lb) which is ten times its weight at

sandwich tern

albatross

herring gull

shag

hatching time. The albatross breeds for the first time when it is ten years old, and in the meantime it makes long journeys across the southern seas. It glides beautifully in the air, but is very clumsy on the ground and has to run to get up enough speed for a take-off.

guillemot

kittiwake

Seabirds nesting on cliff ledges.

little auk

immature
white ibis

white ibis

scarlet ibis

The Mangrove Swamps

Mangrove swamps are found on certain parts of the coast in tropical regions: in northern South America, in central America, parts of Africa, southern Asia, Malaysia and Australasia. They consist of trees which form a kind of forest growing in salty mud and are bathed twice a day by seawater at the bases of their trunks. Aerial roots grow out from the trunk and branches of a mangrove. These hang down into water and mud. The animal life in the mangrove swamps includes both land and water animals. In South America big colonies of birds settle in the trees. The scarlet ibis, a magnificent bird which is completely scarlet except for four large wing-feathers tipped with dark blue, nests in Venezuela, Colombia, the Guianas, the north-east of Brazil and in Trinidad. A few of this species wander as far as the Antilles and even Florida. Colonies of ibis often settle in mangrove swamps and mingle with groups of other birds such as the white ibis, the egret and the spoonbill. Its only predators appear to be a rat and two species of birds – the buzzard and the cuckoo which steal its eggs.

The scarlet ibis catches crabs, molluscs, insects, including fly larvae and aquatic bugs, and small fishes. In Trinidad it builds its nest between 4 and 10 m (13–33 ft) above the water,

A mangrove swamp at high tide.

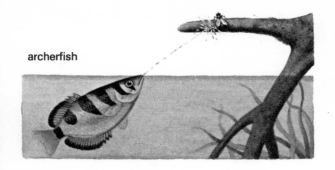

archerfish

while in Surinam the nests are rarely found more than 1.5 m (5 ft) above the water. Made of dry branches and lined with leaves, they measure about 30 cm (12 in) across and are firmly fixed in the fork of a tree. Most nests only last for one season.

One of the strangest fishes to be found in the mangrove swamps, other than the climbing perch, which has been wrongly said to climb actually into the branches of trees, is the archerfish. This has a very special hunting technique. Staying just below the surface of the water, it watches for insects which land on the plants overhanging the water's edge. If it sees one within a reasonable distance – between 1 m and 1.5 m (3–5 ft) – it pushes its snout out of the water and shoots a jet of water in the direction of the insect. The insect is knocked off the plant and the fish swallows it. The young archerfishes, which are about 3 cm (1¼ in) long,

are able to shoot down insects at a closer range than the adult. The fish positions itself as close as possible beneath its victim and fixes it in its sights. Then it swallows a little water and compresses it quickly between the tongue and a groove in its palate. This groove leads into an

horsehoe crab or king crab

fiddler crab

extremely small tube. The fish then pokes its nose above the surface of the water and fires. The insects are hit from below and fall into the water. The maximum firing range is ten times the length of the fish. There are four or five species of archerfishes in the mangrove swamps of the Philippines, Vietnam, Indonesia and the nearby island of Malacca.

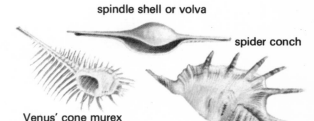

spindle shell or volva

spider conch

Venus' cone murex

cleaner fish

filefish

grunts

soft coral

lionfish or dragonfi

clown fish

stony coral

sea-anemone

butterfly fish

brain stone coral

Coral Seas

In the tropics the surface temperature of the sea never falls much below 18°C (62°F), a very favourable environment for corals, which over a long period of time form colonies. These in turn build up into islands and strings of coral reefs. The Great Barrier Reef, off the eastern coast of Australia, stretches for a distance of more than 2,000 km (1,250 miles) and consists of thousands of coral islets. Corals also play an important role in the formation of atolls in Oceania, in the Pacific Ocean. An atoll is a circle of coral reef and islands around a central lagoon.

The species of corals differ widely. The colonies can be distinguished not just by their shape but also by the depth at which they grow. Corals which form reefs are as hard as stone and made up of the calcareous skeletons of tiny animals called polyps. These are about 10–12 mm ($\frac{3}{8}$–$\frac{1}{2}$ in) long. Like their relatives, the sea-anemones, they have stinging cells. After the animals die, their skeletons remain, and new polyps establish themselves on top. This is how the reef grows in height and in length, increasing at the rate of 5–28 mm every year, and sometimes more.

Coral reefs are the home of many other animals. Some, such as the parrotfishes, feed on the polyps. Worms, sea-anemones and molluscs attach themselves to the coral. Among the permanent inhabitants are the giant clams, well known for their size and their interesting

structure. One of them is the biggest bivalve mollusc in the world – it grows to a length of 1.2 m (4 ft), a width of 60 cm (2 ft), a height of 60 cm (2 ft) and weighs up to 260 kg (570 lb). The smallest of the six giant clam species, which are spread over the Indian and Pacific Oceans and the Red Sea, never grows any bigger than 15 cm (6 in).

Many of the fishes on coral reefs are brightly coloured. Angelfishes and butterfly fishes are striped or spotted with black, orange, red, yellow and blue.

Like mammals and birds, fishes often have parasites living on their skin which trouble them. If they cannot get rid of them by rubbing their bodies against rocks or coral, they sometimes present themselves to certain small fishes which take on the task of removing the parasites.

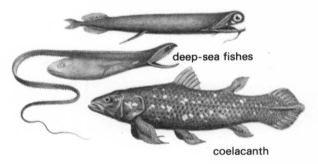

deep-sea fishes

coelacanth

These 'cleaner fishes' do not all belong to the same family. One such fish, the wrasse waits in a hole in a rock for its customers to come to it, and then gets on with the job. The wrasse swallows the parasites and the bits of dead skin from fishes such as rays, butterfly fishes and parrotfishes.

There are 250 species of sharks, the smallest of which grow no bigger than 40 cm (16 in). Until now, only 29 species have attacked humans or boats, but there are two which are particularly dangerous. These are the great white shark or man-eater and the mako shark. The great white shark is common in all warm seas. Its triangular-shaped teeth may grow to a height of 5 cm (2 in).

The swordfish is a deep-sea fish (pelagic). It lays its eggs in waters with a temperature of not less than 23°C (72°F).

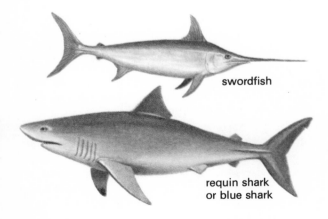

swordfish

requin shark
or blue shark

Shallow Seas

From the shoreline the sea-bed slopes down gradually to a depth of between 180 and 200 m (600–650 ft). This is called the continental shelf, because it is an extension of the continent. At the seaweed edge of this shelf is a steep slope where the sea-bed drops rapidly to depths of between 3,000 and 6,500 m (2–4 miles), with here and there mountains, the tops of which appear above the surface and are known as islands, or which are below the surface and are called sea mounts.

In the Pacific Ocean there are submarine troughs or trenches which may be as much as 10,000 m (6 miles) below the surface. The Atlantic Ocean reaches a depth of 8,300 m (5 miles) between Africa and America, but between France and Great Britain the English Channel is only 200 m (650 ft) deep.

In the depths of the seas and oceans live about 180,000 species of animals. Nearer to the surface can be found plankton, cetaceans (whales, dolphins and porpoises) and many fishes, both on their own and in schools. The few birds on the open seas are mostly puffins, petrels and guillemots, for the gulls do not generally venture far from the coast.

In winter the continental shelf is the area richest in fish, for most of them go there to lay their eggs. In the shallower waters live the sand-eels, which partially bury themselves in the sand using their spoon-shaped lower jaw like a spade.

The sole is one of the flat fishes. The eyes of the adult are situated on one side of its body. The young sole is like any other fish, but as it grows up, one of its eyes moves over its head, from the left side to the right side, and comes to rest close to the other one. At the same time its body becomes flatter.

The sting ray is a coastal fish found particularly in the Mediterranean. It is a ray and therefore has a cartilaginous skeleton like a shark. Halfway along its long, slender tail is a poisonous spike with which it can inflict very painful injuries.

The John Dory or St Peter's fish has a very high but narrow body and feeds almost entirely on small fishes. In the stomach of one John Dory were found two sand-eels, eighteen sprats and an octopus. This fish lives in the English Channel, the North Sea, the Atlantic and the Mediterranean. Its name comes from the black spot surrounded by yellow. A legend tells us it is the mark left by Saint Peter on the one he caught in the Sea of Galilee containing the tribute money.

There are two other fishes on rocky coasts which are similar in shape and in their carnivorous habits. These are the conger and the moray eel. The conger is different from the ordinary freshwater eel because it is scaleless, and also because it is exclusively marine. The largest reach a length of 3 m (10 ft) and weigh up to 65 kg (145 lb).

The moray eel is used to the warm waters of the Mediterranean and hides in the crevices of rocks or holes in the wreckage of ships. It feeds on fish and crustaceans. It has a formidable appearance with its strangely shaped head, its vicious-looking teeth and its staring eyes (in fact, all fish have unblinking eyes and are unable to close them because they do not have eyelids). In its mouth are glands which secrete poison when the fish bites. Other species of moray eel live in tropical seas.

The gurnard is a very strange-looking fish. Three rays of each of its pectoral fins are like fingers and help the fish to move along and disturb the sand so that it can find its food. It has a swimbladder, a bag full of gas, which keeps it at a certain depth in the water and prevents it from going any deeper.

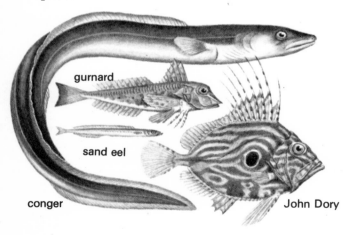

gurnard

sand eel

conger

John Dory

Underwater scene around a rocky reef.

moray eel

sting ray

jewfish
or grouper

sole

Basking shark swimming slowly forward with open mouth to sieve small animals from the sea.

Temperate Seas

About three-quarters of the surface of the world is covered by oceans. This figure represents an enormous volume of salt water. Thousands of little animals and plants float about with the currents close to the surface. They are called plankton. Most of the animals found in plankton are only just visible to the naked eye and are more or less transparent, but jellyfishes are bigger. Many jellyfish measure between 20 and 30 cm (8–12 in) across, and in the north Atlantic Ocean there is a species which is over 1 m (3 ft) across, with tentacles 20 m (65 ft) long.

Diatoms are microscopic algae. With the spores of brown and green algae, they make up much of the plant plankton on which the animal plankton feeds. The animal plankton is eaten by fishes like sardines and sand-eels, which in their turn are food for carnivorous species (the conger and the moray eel). There are also some very large fishes which feed on plankton. One of these is the harmless whale shark, which may have as many as 15,000 tiny teeth yet feeds on minute shrimps and small squids in the plankton, as does the basking shark.

Plant plankton lives near the surface, where it can receive the sunlight. Some animal plankton, on the other hand, moves up and down in the water – at night it moves up to the surface and in the daytime stays at a depth of between 50 and 800 m (165–2,600 ft). Plankton is less abundant in winter than in summer. As the days shorten, many animals and seaweeds disappear. Their decaying bodies enrich the seawater with minerals and organic substances. In the spring, as the days lengthen, the plant and animal plankton populations increase again.

There are several species of tunny-fish. In the Atlantic and the Mediterranean the biggest is the tunny or blue fin tuna. The French call it red tunny because of the red colour of its flesh. Tunny or tuna are strong swimmers and travel

Plankton is made up of thousands of minute plants and animals.

a long way. They have nine small finlets on both back and underside, just in front of their tail fin. Little is known about their movements, but the Californian tunny, with its silver stripes, has been caught off Japan, having travelled distances of more than 7,500 kilometres. This is one of those rare species of fishes whose body temperature can rise higher than that of the surrounding water. The tunny lays up to 10 million eggs.

The cod lives in cold seas over a wide area extending as far as and beyond the Arctic Circle. It lives with many others of its kind, all about the same size, in shoals. The young stay together in groups separate from the shoals of older fish. The cod and some related species like haddock have a sort of beard on the chin called a barbel.

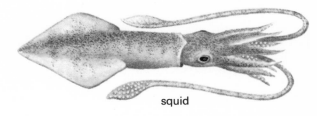

squid

Squids are invertebrates which live in the open sea. They are related to octopuses, but they have eight relatively short tentacles and two longer arms covered in suckers, with which they capture their prey. These molluscs have two horizontal, triangular-shaped fins and a large head with big eyes. They are called cephalopods (from two Greek words meaning 'head' and 'foot') because their tentacles, which although they are called arms take the place of a foot, branch out of their head. Squids vary in size from 10 to 60 cm (4–24 in), but there are

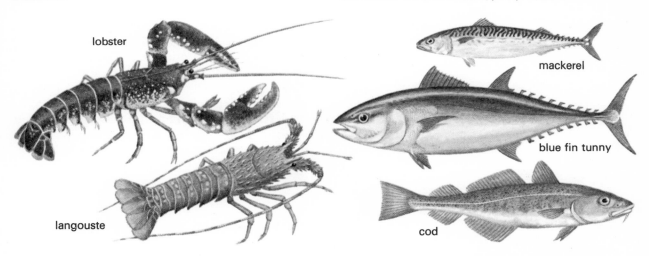

lobster

langouste

mackerel

blue fin tunny

cod

The mackerel lives in shoals. It is easy to identify because its back is banded blue and dark green. It lives in the Mediterranean, on both sides of the Atlantic, in the English Channel, the North Sea and the Baltic.

Several species of shark live in temperate waters, but none is really dangerous. In tropical waters, however, there are many, including man-eating species. Sharks differ from other fishes like the tunny, in having a skeleton of cartilage, or gristle, not bone. They breathe like other fishes by means of gills, but whereas the gills of bony fishes are covered by an operculum, or gill-cover, in sharks the gills are connected to the outside by five to seven vertical slits.

some giant squids which live in deep water. One, which was washed up on a beach in New Zealand was 6 m (20 ft) long (head and body) and 13 m (43 ft) total length. Squid and cuttlefish have a sort of shell inside their body. In squid, it is horny, small and feather-shaped, but the cuttlefish shell is bigger, contains a lot of lime and is called cuttlebone.

Most rays, as well as dogfish, which are small sharks, lay eggs in a rectangular horny case or capsule. At each corner is a tendril which wraps around seaweed and anchors the egg-case, so that it is not washed away.

The lobster and crayfish are two big shellfish which live in our seas.

Tropical Seas

Birds are often thought to fly faster than they really do, because people forget to take account of the force of the wind. This can either push them along or slow them down. Frigatebirds, large birds found in the Indian, Pacific and Atlantic Oceans, are reputed to be able to fly at a speed of 300 km (200 miles) per hour, but in fact they only reach this speed if they are being carried along by a gale. In calm weather the magnificent frigatebird flies at 20 to 25 km (12–15 miles) per hour. It nests in colonies and builds its nest on bushes 1 to 1.5 m (3–5 ft) above the ground. Because it has such long wings, it needs a lift to help get it into the air for take-off. A gust of wind has the desired effect.

The frigatebird lays only one egg and the young bird flies from the nest when it is about 165 days old, although its parents keep on feeding it for four months. The frigatebird has a clever way of getting much of its food – it pursues other sea-birds, such as gannets, gulls

masked booby

fairy tern

noddy tern

and terns, and makes them drop their catch. The frigatebird is also quite capable of catching its own food.

There are at least forty-eight species of sea snakes throughout the warm zones of the Pacific and Indian Oceans, especially around Malaysia. They all secrete a very strong venom. The only one that can be called pelagic is the yellow-bellied sea snake, for it lives in the open sea far from the coast, while the others do not move out farther than 5 or 6 km (3–3¾ miles).

Several species of turtle live in the sea. They are the green turtle, the hawksbill turtle and the leathery turtle or leatherback, which is the biggest. Turtles are reptiles with short legs and a shell formed of bony plates which are attached to the vertebral column and to the sides of the animal. The shell is like a box with holes for the turtle's limbs and head. All turtles lay eggs with a white shell which is like parchment. The eggs are incubated by the heat of the sun or by the heat generated by decaying vegetable matter, such as leaves and branches.

The legs of sea turtles are like oars or paddles. The leathery turtle does not have such a rigid shell and this is covered with a leathery skin. It lives on its own in the Atlantic, Pacific and Indian Oceans. Mating takes place in the water, then every year at the same time (May to June in Sri Lanka) the females lay their eggs on the quiet beaches. Once out of the water, they make their way slowly over the sand, leaving long dragging tracks behind them. Each female digs a hole and in it lays between 30 and 120 eggs. Then she covers up the hole and goes back to the sea. Egg-laying always takes place at night. Each female lays about four batches of eggs each season. Two months later, the baby turtles hatch out. Hatching takes place at night, but the baby turtles leave the nest by day and have to cover the distance between the nest and the water as quickly as possible, otherwise they may fall prey to the gulls, frigatebirds and crabs. Many are caught before they can reach the water and become food for their animal captors.

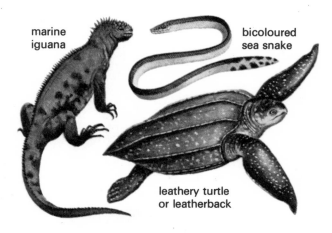

marine iguana

bicoloured sea snake

leathery turtle or leatherback

Nesting colony of frigate birds with a white chick on the nest. In the breeding season the males have a brilliant red throat pouch which they display in courtship.

The Arctic

The Arctic zone extends right around the North Pole and covers about 25 million sq km (10 million sq miles). This is more than forty times the surface area of the British Isles. It includes the extreme north of Asia, America and Europe as well as the frozen seas which in winter form the Great Ice Barrier of islands and stretches of permanent ice. The conditions to which living creatures in this region are subjected are so rigorous that the slightest change in climate, such as a delay in the melting of the ice in spring, may cause the death of hundreds of thousands of birds and other animals. Because of the low temperatures and the short summer, the number of species is small. However, 119 species of plants have been counted on Devon Island to the north of Canada.

In the Arctic region there are several mammals and birds which have white fur or feathers all the year long. They are the glaucous gull, the snow goose, the gyrfalcon and the polar bear. The ptarmigan, the ermine, or stoat and the wolf, however, are white only in winter.

The polar bear readily takes to the water, al-though it spends the greater part of its life on land or on the ice. Polar bears seldom wander far from the coast. In spring and summer they are carried south by the ice as far as the tundra. They are perfectly equipped to withstand the cold because, underneath their fur, is a layer of insulating fat. Their ears are short and the pads on their feet are hairy. They are good swimmers. Their favourite prey is seals. They also eat dead fish and other carrion and nestling birds.

The female polar bear gives birth to two young (only one if it is her first year of breeding) in a den which she makes in the autumn by

narwhal

beluga or
white whale

A group of walrus, a harp seal with her baby and a polar bear on ice floes in the Arctic.

digging a hole in a mass of frozen snow. The bear cubs weigh only 750 gm (26 oz) when they are born in January and their eyes do not open until they are one month old. At three months they are weaned and follow their mother about and stay with her for at least a year.

The walrus is found only in the Arctic regions. Its limbs are big flippers. It has a rounded shape, very short ears and a thick layer of fat or blubber under the skin. It can be recognized by its very long tusks formed by the upper canine teeth. It uses these to scrape the sea-bottom for bivalve molluscs and sea-snails, or to hoist itself up on to the ice.

The beluga and the narwhal are two whales of the Arctic seas. The beluga is also known as the white whale, but the young are grey. It lives close to the coast and sometimes travels great distances up rivers. It catches fish that live in shoals, squid and crustaceans.

The narwhal was once thought of as a mythical animal because the long spirally-twisted tusk on the head of the male looks like the horn of the unicorn. It is in fact an upper canine made of ivory.

walrus
harp seal
ringed seal
snow goose
Ross's gull
fulmar

Antarctica

In contrast to the Arctic, which consists of a frozen ocean with scattered islands, the Antarctic is a proper continent covered with a thick layer of ice which may be up to 4,000 m ($2\frac{1}{2}$ miles) thick. The vegetation is very poor and there is no tundra, like that which borders the Arctic Ocean. Only two species of flowering plants have been found there, but there are 400 species of lichens, 10 fungi and 72 species of mosses on the edges of the continent. There are very few insects and other land invertebrates. The sea, on the other hand, is teeming with life. Tiny one-celled algae, called diatoms are food for several species of shrimp which are up to 7.5 cm (3 in) long. In a mass, these shrimps are called krill. Colonies of penguins, as well as the most common seals and whales, depend on the krill for food. They in turn are a prey to carnivores such as the killer whale and the leopard seal. Thus, without these little crustaceans the other animals would not be able to live.

There are ten species of bird which nest on the Antarctic continent and nine others nest on the large peninsula which extends from it. Skuas, relatives of gulls but brown in colour, have been seen passing over a research station 1,200 km (750 miles) from the coast and at an altitude of 3,000 m (1,000 ft), in an area where the lowest recorded temperature is $-52°C$ ($-61°F$). Dead animals and plants decompose very slowly in the Antarctic because it is so cold. Similarly, the ground covering of lichens and mosses, in places where it has been destroyed

emperor penguin

by man, will need two or three centuries to grow back again, while the vegetation in temperate lands will recover completely in a few years.

Out of seventeen species of penguins, there are only two, the Adélie penguin and the emperor penguin, which breed on the Antarctic continent itself, and three which nest on the peninsula. The others nest on the islands which surround the continent, and farther north on the southern coasts of Africa, South America and Australia. There are no penguins living in the Northern Hemisphere, although the auks and guillemots of the cold northern seas are often mistaken for penguins.

The emperor penguin, the biggest of all, is the only bird to breed regularly in the middle of winter. It is an extremely sociable bird and lives in colonies, the largest of which contains about 100,000 birds. In total, there are probably over 300,000 emperor penguins in 22 colonies. Breeding begins in March. Mating takes place over a period of about a month, and during this time both male and female go without food, because they stay in one place and their only food is to be found in the sea.

The female lays one egg, which she hands over to the male. He keeps it on top of his feet and covers it with a fold of abdominal skin. Thus the egg is kept very warm, away from the wind which sometimes blows up to 100 km (60 miles) per hour. The male incubates the egg for 62 days, standing packed in between neighbouring birds to keep warm. When the female returns from the sea, the male is thin because he has had nothing to eat for 90 to 100 days and has lost 30–45% of his original body weight. The baby bird which has just hatched, is kept warm by its mother and receives its first meal. The male goes to the sea to feed, although to do this he must cover a considerable distance. Then the parents begin their search for food for their baby, going to and from the sea. The young bird is fed about fourteen times in $4\frac{1}{2}$ months.

The great skua preys on very young penguins, and feeds on any dead birds washed up by the sea. This is the only bird that nests in both the Arctic and the Antarctic.

The killer whale is a toothed whale. On its back is a triangular fin, 1.6 m (5 ft) high in males. This animal is found in all oceans, but

Adélie penguin

great skua

is most common in cold and temperate seas where it can find its favourite prey – seals, sealions, fish and squid.

The leopard seal or sea leopard differs from other seals in its elongated shape, its relatively thin body and its clearly defined neck.

killer whale

snow petrel

sea leopard

The Weddell seal is a champion diver, and goes down as deep as 350 m (1,150 ft). In the winter it makes holes in the ice through which to breathe. It does this with its teeth, and in old animals the teeth are very well worn.

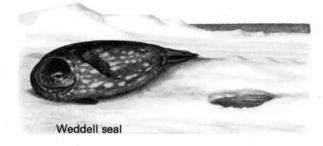

Weddell seal

The Tundra

In northern Europe, Asia and America is a region called the tundra, lying between the taiga and the Arctic Ocean. Its characteristic features are the absence of normal-sized trees and the scarcity of animal life. The winter there lasts for nine months and for several of these the sun lies hidden below the horizon or there is at most a weak sunshine. For the few weeks of summer, however, there is no real night. The ground is frozen to a very great depth – 600 m (2,000 ft) in parts of Alaska – and only the surface warms up in the summer. This is the region of permafrost – permanently frozen – hence the formation of countless lakes and swamps. These are ideal conditions for different species of mosquito, which multiply at an extraordinary rate. These insects are able to live on vegetable juices, so the lack of large mammals whose blood they normally feed on does not worry them.

Plants in the tundra hardly ever grow any higher than 30 to 40 cm (12–16 in). The most common plants are mosses and lichens (477 species in the north of Russia in Nova Zembla), grasses, tiny bushes closely related to the bilberry and dwarf willows and birch trees. Cotton grass, the seeds of which have plumes of white silk like tufts of cotton, is found in the peaty ground so common in the tundra.

The mosquitoes are eaten by many migratory birds which come to the tundra to breed during the short summer (June to August). There are waders (sandpipers, phalaropes, curlews, golden plovers), web-footed birds (gulls, skuas, ducks, terns) and perching birds (willow warblers, chats, Lapland buntings). These birds have just enough time to build a nest, lay and incubate their eggs and raise their young before the first snow begins to fall in the second half of August.

In winter the ptarmigan, the rough-legged buzzard, the gyrfalcon and the raven are the biggest non-migratory birds. Neither reptiles

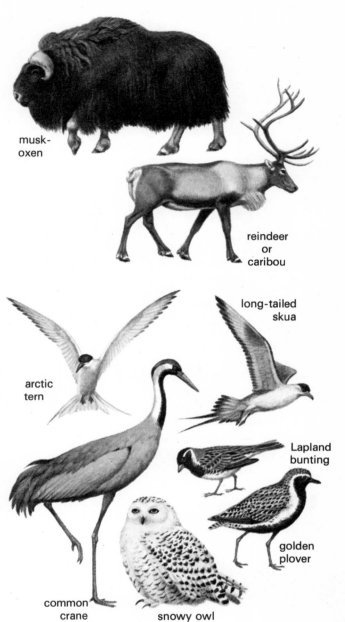

Left: Arctic fox hunting a lemming. The fox is still in winter coat, although the snow has just melted and the spring flowers are blooming. In summer it will have a brown coat.

nor amphibians are to be found living in the tundra, and the number of invertebrate species is small.

The arctic fox has a very soft white coat which changes colour to brown and white in the summer. It eats anything it can find – in summer, lemmings and fieldmice, birds and eggs; in winter it follows the polar bear and the wolf and eats the remains of their kill.

Lemmings are small rodents well known for the way they periodically increase enormously in numbers. Every four or five years their numbers build up and then disappear after a few months, except for the odd one which remains. This is a phenomenon which happens regularly and which still puzzles scientists. Predators such as the snowy owl and the skua make the most of the increased population of lemmings and lay more eggs (the owl lays up to ten instead of the usual three to six) because there is more food for their young. In years

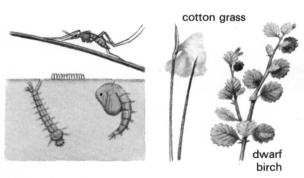

Above left: Mosquito, with raft of eggs and a larva and a pupa under water.

when the lemmings are few, the carnivores breed very little, if at all, or else they migrate south. All sorts of stories are told about the lemmings – one is that they commit suicide in the rivers or in the sea. Observation has shown that this is a false idea. However abundant they are, the lemmings move in the spring and, in crossing watercourses, a certain number of them are drowned. These are accidental deaths rather than suicides.

The arctic tern is one of the greatest travellers in the bird world. After nesting in the tundra, it migrates south to spend the winter in the Southern Hemisphere, covering a distance of 30,000 or 40,000 km (20,000–25,000 miles) per year.

The common crane nests in the tundra of the Scandinavian plateaus and especially on the edge of the taiga. It is the biggest European wading bird.

The Taiga

Taiga is the name given to the huge forest-land of pines, spruce, fir and larch which extends south of the tundra across Europe, Siberia and Canada. Growing with the conifers are poplars, aspens and birch trees. It is, therefore, a forest of mixed trees which do not grow very big because of the cold climate. The snow covers the ground from October to May.

birch   bilberry   lichen

The undergrowth here consists of berry-producing bushes. Many different kinds of lichen hang from the branches and others such as the reindeer moss, or cladonia cover almost all the surface of the ground. With its forests, its marshes and its rivers, such as the Lena, the Ob and the Mackenzie, the taiga is much richer in flora and fauna than the tundra because it offers shelter in winter. The trees act as a vast wind-break and once inside the forest hardly a breeze can be detected. A wind helps to lower the temperature of the atmosphere very quickly, and by escaping it, the reindeer and birds have more chance of surviving the low temperatures which can reach −60°C (−76°F) in Siberia. Some sparrows actually bury themselves in a hole in the snow and stay there for the night.

The brown bear is the largest carnivore in the taiga. It feeds on insects and their larvae, rodents, eggs, fruit, grasses, honey, and the dead bodies of animals. In short, it will eat almost anything. In the spring, in Alaska, the grizzly bear, which is a very large brown bear, fishes for salmon which are swimming upstream to their breeding grounds. In winter the bear retires to a hole in a rock or under the roots of a fallen tree, and falls into a half-sleep. The bear may live for twenty-five or thirty years.

The largest of the deer family, the elk is called the moose in America. It is an excellent swimmer, and can cross lakes and wide stretches of water. It finds some of its food (grasses, leaves, stems and bark) by the water's edge. Its large hoofs enable it to make its way across the thick blanket of snow which is sometimes as much as 60 cm (2 ft) deep.

Wolves often separate a young elk or deer from the adults and kill it. The wolf has been

Young wapiti (known in Britain as a red deer) being chased by wolves.

exterminated in many parts of the world but many remain in Russia and Siberia (about 50,000) and in Alaska (about 20,000). There are only about twenty left in Scandinavia. They very rarely attack man, even in the winter when they are hungry. In the taiga and on the edge of the tundra, wolves eat fieldmice, hares, ducks that are moulting so cannot fly, wild boar, roe deer and farm animals (goats, calves, sheep, dogs and pigs). They follow herds of reindeer

hawk owl

Siberian jay

goshawk

lynx

wapiti

brown bear

or wapitis (American deer) in the autumn in the hope that they can capture a lame or weak animal.

The goshawk is widespread in the taiga and evergreen forests. Although it is fairly small, it is one of the most powerful birds of prey, along with the peregrine falcon. Its prey consists mostly of such birds as crows, jays, pigeons and thrushes, as well as small mammals, such as young hares.

Birds of prey and carnivorous mammals have a very important role in nature because they keep down the numbers of the animals on which they feed. Other factors controlling animal populations are parasites, sickness, bad weather and lack of food.

35

Plants of the Temperate Grasslands of Europe

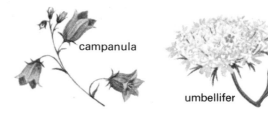

campanula

umbellifer

Meadow grasslands, covered with grasses and other small plants, are found near rivers. The dampness there, unsuitable for many trees, encourages the growth of the grass.

Meadows like this can be found in the mountains as well as on the plains, but the plants that grow in these two situations are not all the same, although they may look similar. The differences between species are in fact not always very obvious. On the plains there are several species of grass to be seen as well as pink, white, yellow and violet flowers which follow one another in season. The number of plant species in our meadows has not increased much. Scarcely more than 60 have been counted overall, while there are about 550 species of animals – insects, spiders, snails and so on.

It is easy to distinguish the grasses from plants like the daisy and campanula. Grasses are green all over and have hollow stems. They also have long, narrow leaves which are pointed at the ends and stiff and sharp on the edges. These leaves fit into the stem at points where it is closed off by a division called a node. At the very end of the stem there appears a spike, a mass of tiny flowers. These do not attract honey-gathering insects such as bees, bumble-bees or certain flies, because they do not have any smell and they are not brightly coloured.

At the beginning of spring, in March or April, the cardamine or cuckooflower blooms in the damp meadows. The daisy comes out

thistles

even earlier, and in places where the winter is mild, it flowers all year round. The ox-eye daisy flowers in June. If you look at it closely, you will see that it is made up of dozens of little tubular yellow flowers, or florets, surrounded by other florets with a sort of white wing. Because the daisy bloom is made up of many tiny flowers or florets, it is called a composite flower.

In the same family of composite flowers are the cornflower, thistles, camomile, arnica and many other species.

The flower is the reproductive organ of most plants. The flower of the buttercup is carried on a stalk, known as the peduncle. It consists of five yellow petals beneath which are five smaller green leaves called sepals. At the base of each petal there is a tiny gland which secretes a sweet liquid. This is called nectar and it is this that brings insects to the flower.

The reproductive organs are grouped in the centre of the flower. They are the carpels (the female organs) and the stamens.

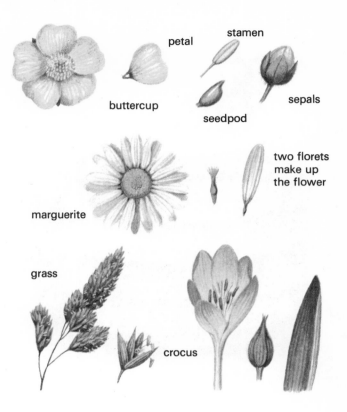

petal
stamen
buttercup
sepals
seedpod
marguerite
two florets make up the flower
grass
crocus

marguerite
campanula

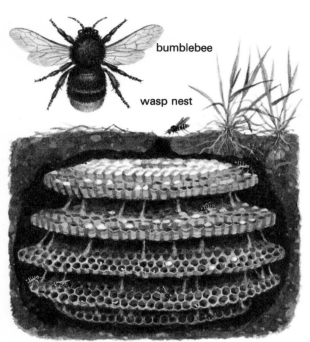

bumblebee

wasp nest

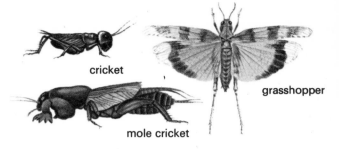

cricket

mole cricket

grasshopper

is their job to collect food and enlarge the nest while the queen is laying. The colony grows until, in the autumn, it contains about a hundred insects. They all die before the onset of winter, except for a few special females, or queens, which spend the cold months without eating, in a crack in the bark of a tree or a crevice in a wall.

The swallowtail, one of the most beautiful butterflies, also undergoes a complete metamorphosis. In June the eggs which have been

Insects of the Temperate Grasslands of Europe

Most of the animal life in the meadows or grass-lands is very small, consisting of insects, spiders and small snails, which either eat the plants or devour each other.

Insects have three pairs of legs. Most of them lay eggs from which hatch larvae. These are either like miniature adults or completely different. If they are different, they must undergo a change called a metamorphosis: the larva stops eating and changes into a pupa (if the insect is a butterfly the pupa is known as a chrysalis). Finally, the adult emerges from the pupa as a perfect insect, known as the imago.

The female bumble bee builds her nest in spring. Glands in her abdomen give out wax with which she makes a kind of cradle, just below ground surface. This is made up of several compartments some of which she fills with honey and pollen, and others where she lays about ten eggs. After these have hatched, the female (or queen) feeds the larvae or grubs. The young bumblebees which come from the grubs are all females. They are the workers. It

laid on the wild carrot, fennel or cow-parsley hatch into caterpillars which feed on these plants. As they eat, they grow bigger and then they must shed their skin because it cannot stretch. The caterpillars have eight pairs of legs and if they are disturbed, they put out two little red horns at the back of their head. Before they change into the chrysalis, they attach themselves to a stem with a silk thread.

Unlike the caterpillar and the butterfly, the chrysalis does not move and does not eat. It spends the whole winter absolutely motionless, and the butterfly emerges in May.

The brown ant is found in meadows, woods and gardens. Ant colonies are made up of several thousand individuals belonging to different groups. First of all there is the queen. She is very big. Then there are smaller females and some males. The males and the queen are the only ones which have wings, between July and August. This is the time when they mate. The nests of these ants can be found under stones or in the ground under a little mound.

Brown ants feed mainly on honeydew, a sweet substance produced by the greenfly. Their eggs are tiny. What are commonly called eggs are in fact unmoving, whitish pupae. Brown ant colonies live a long time because these insects

do not die off in the winter. Some ants have a sting at the very end of their body, while others defend themselves by biting.

The cuckoo spit owes its name to the blob of foam which hides its larvae and which looks like spittle. The larva produces it by blowing air into its liquid, soapy excrement. Then it adds a special substance to stop it from drying out. Throughout the whole of this operation the insect hangs upside down.

The cricket, the green grasshopper and the bush cricket 'sing' with a harsh, monotonous sort of sound. They are classed together because they are alike in build and habits.

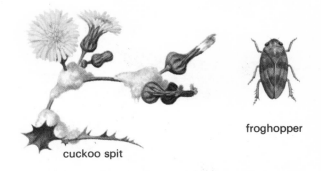

cuckoo spit

froghopper

Swallowtail butterflies with their caterpillars and a chrysalis on the plants.

brown ant

Birds of the Temperate Grasslands of Europe

The number of birds living in grassland is not great compared with the number found in wooded areas. But meadows offer a feeding ground for a number of species belonging to other habitats.

Grey wagtails are at home near streams, seldom going far from the water's edge. These

curlew

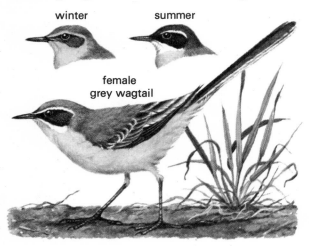

winter   summer

female
grey wagtail

carrion crow

little birds are called wagtails from the way they wag their tails when moving about on the ground. Grey wagtails winter in Africa, returning to Europe in April. They can be seen perching on fences and plants which are strong enough to support their weight. The pattern of colours on the head changes from winter to summer.

The curlew with its long curved beak feeds on mud-flats and marshes and nests on moors, meadows and marshes. This bird makes little in the way of a nest. It lays its four eggs on the

ground. As soon as the chicks hatch, covered in down, they are able to trot along with their parents.

You might see a bird perched on a hedge or on a tall bush at the edge of a meadow, which looks as though it is keeping watch. It is a red-backed shrike or male butcher-bird. The female has a more sombre plumage than the male, of buff and brown. The shrike is carnivorous, or meat-eating, and lives on large insects such as cockchafers and wasps. It may also eat field-mice, frogs and more rarely small birds. It is

40

whinchat

The red-backed shrike sometimes impales its prey on thorns.

called a butcher-bird because it has the curious habit of impaling its prey on thorns. This makes it easier for the bird to dismember its prey, but the habit is not very common amongst the members of this species.

The carrion crow is likely to be seen anywhere except deep in a forest. It is a familiar sight in newly-mown fields, with its quaint strutting walk. If you see one of these birds, there is likely to be another not far away. In fact, it is one of the few birds in which male and female keep together nearly all the year round.

In summer carrion crows form groups of about ten birds. They are about the same size and colour as rooks, but do not have the grey skin around the base of the beak, which distinguishes a rook.

Male hen harrier passing food to the female hen harrier in mid-air.

Prairies of North and South America

The white man has turned the natural prairies of most of North America into farmland. In the mountainous regions of the west, however, the land remains much the same, except that the large animals called bison or buffalo, which used to roam there now live in protected reserves, and the pronghorn antelope, which still lives wild, is fewer in numbers than it used to be. Other smaller species, such as prairiedogs and prairie chickens, are also much fewer than they used to be and will survive only if strictly protected. On the other hand, predators like the coyote and the puma have resisted the changes and are still numerous, particularly the coyote.

The American bison, usually called the buffalo, can be distinguished from its cousin, the European bison or wisent, by the very long thick hair on its head and forequarters. Moreover, it holds its head lower than the European bison. The females in both species are smaller and lighter than the males.

There are two subspecies of American bison: the forest bison and the plains bison which, up until the nineteenth century lived in enormous herds. It is estimated that 50 million bison must have roamed the American plains at one time. They migrated regularly, moving in autumn towards the south to find better feeding grounds. In 1889 there were, however, 560 left, all the others having been senselessly massacred. By strict conservation their numbers have now built up to about 25,000.

buffalo or
American bison

American
sparrowhawk

coyote

prairiedog

greater prairie
chicken

pronghorn

Pronghorns live only in North America. They are somewhere between deer and cattle: their branched horns are shed every year like those of deer, but the bony cores of the horns are permanent, as in cattle. They can be found from the Missouri to the Rocky Mountains and from Mexico to Canada. The pronghorn is the fastest American mammal, able to reach a speed of 80 km (50 miles) per hour over short distances.

Despite their name, prairiedogs are rodents related to woodchucks. They used to be widespread throughout the west of the United States. They are extremely sociable animals, living in colonies known as towns, in which there are many burrows, each occupied by a family. The prairiedog eats grasses and insects.

The coyote resembles the jackal of the Old World in its life style and its appearance. It hunts hares, rabbits, prairiedogs, small rodents, birds, lizards, and insects and also likes carrion and fruit.

In South America the prairies are called by different names depending on the country. In Venezuela and Brazil they are called savannah and are dotted with clumps of trees; in Uruguay and Argentina they are known as pampas, most of which has only recently been cultivated. There one can see flightless birds called rheas. These are like the ostriches that live on the African savannah and the emu that lives on the Australian grasslands. The two species of rheas, the biggest of which stands up to 1.5 m (5 ft) tall and weighs up to 25 kg (55 lb), both have feathers all over their heads, with no bare skin showing through. The male alone incubates the eggs. There are twenty to thirty eggs laid by several females in a huge nest. If there are more eggs, he is unable to keep all of them warm and some of them go bad.

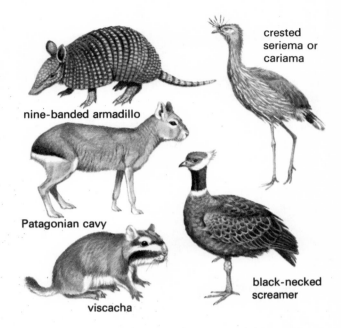

nine-banded armadillo

crested seriema or cariama

Patagonian cavy

viscacha

black-necked screamer

The crested seriema looks like the African secretary bird, but is a relative of the rails. The black-necked screamer is related to the goose and has some strange characteristics, including a horny spur on its wing.

rheas

The African Savannah

African
elephant

The lion lives in Africa south of the Sahara and in the Forest of Gir in India, north of Bombay, where there are now only 200 left. It has become extinct in North Africa, and in the rest of the African continent it is found mainly in game reserves.

The lion is the most social of all the big cats. It lives in groups of up to twenty animals called prides, which are usually made up of a male,

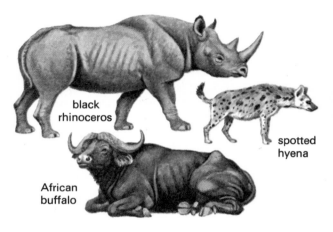

black
rhinoceros

spotted
hyena

African
buffalo

lion

gazelles

several lionesses and their cubs. The lion cubs, between one and five in a litter, are weaned at seven or eight months, but do not begin to hunt on their own until they are sixteen months to two years old. However, many of them die before reaching this age, from lack of food. The lion cubs have to be content with what is left of the kill after the adults have finished with it. Some cubs are killed by leopards or hyenas, and others are abandoned. The only enemies of the adult lions are man and other lions with whom they sometimes fight to the death. The young males leave the pride at the age of eighteen months to two years, but do not become adults until they are three to four years old. The females, on the other hand, stay in the pride and usually spend their whole life there.

Lions hunt alone, in twos or in a group, and the females catch more prey than the males. They eat an average of 6 to 7 kg (13–15 lb) of meat per day, but often have to live off it for a week or more.

The lion is far from being successful every time in the hunt and often has nothing to eat. He must sometimes make do with animals that have been killed by hyenas.

The cheetah is very different from the lion in the way it hunts. It is a spotted wild cat and

giraffe

is becoming more and more rare: there are only 10,000 to 20,000 left in Africa, and in Asia it is even scarcer. When it has located its prey, the leopard approaches stealthily, hiding behind bushes and hillocks. When it is about 100 m (300 ft) away, it races towards the animal in order to catch it. In so doing, it may reach a speed of 90 km (55 miles) per hour and sometimes even 110 km (68 miles) per hour.

One cheetah uses a termite hill as a look-out post while another creeps forward towards a gazelle it has picked out for its victim.

cheetah

zebras

The African Savannah

Between the Sahara desert and the tropical forests of East and Central Africa stretches the savannah – vast prairies covered with tall grass. In East Africa the tallest variety, called 'elephant grass' reaches a height of 3 m (10 ft). These savannahs are dotted with bushes and trees – acacias with spines 10 cm (4 in) long

baobab   acacia

and baobabs, the density of which varies according to the rainfall. The baobab has a very thick trunk. It can measure as much as 20 or 30 m (65–100 ft) in girth for a height of

only 20 or 25 m (65–80 ft). In these areas of grassland there is a dry season, which lasts two and a half to seven months, and a wet season, during which the vegetation grows and numerous birds breed. Grasslands cover more than a third of Africa.

Because there are very few hiding places, or cover, and few watering places, many grassland animals are excellent runners or walkers, not only able to escape their enemies but to cover great distances in search of water or green pastures. Some twenty-five species of large herbivorous mammals live on the savannahs, and fewer than a dozen carnivores depend on them for food. Although there are so many different species, there is little competition for food between them because they do not all have the same diet. Besides, they do not always frequent the same places. The herbivores graze at different levels depending on their size: the dik-diks, for example, tiny antelopes about 35 cm (14 in) high, cannot feed on the leaves of trees as the tall giraffe can. The animals of the savannah can withstand dryness

Ruppell's griffon

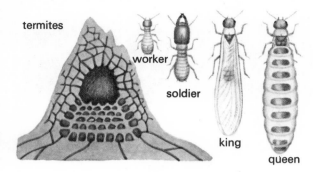

termites
worker
soldier
king
queen

length and 2.5 cm (1 in) in diameter for her abdomen is swollen with eggs. She is thought to live fifty years, which is a record amongst insects. She lays up to 30,000 or even 40,000 eggs per day. Termites live on cellulose, which is the substance making up the framework of all vegetation, as well as fungi, which they grow in their nests and which help to digest the cellulose.

The ostrich is the largest living bird in the

and heat as well as the great differences in temperature between day and night. Temperatures can vary from 40°C (104°F) in the shade at midday to 3°C (38°F) just before dawn.

Crickets, ant and termites are the most numerous insects. Most termites live hidden in the wood of trees or in the ground, but some build mounds, called termite hills or termitaria which are 2 or 3 m (6–10 ft) high and sometimes up to 6 m. Termites are social insects, the most numerous of which are those known as Macrotermes, which build nests above ground and dig very long tunnels underground. Each termite colony consists of several castes: the

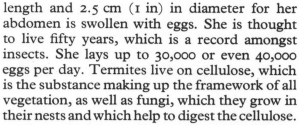

secretary bird
weaverbird
ground hornbill
marabou
ostrich

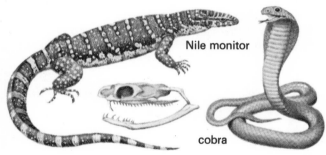

Nile monitor
cobra

queen and king, and usually several kinds of soldiers. The soldiers and workers are blind and wingless. The workers are in charge of the maintenance and construction work of the nest. They also stock the nest with food, while the soldiers are responsible for defending it. Termites shun the light and avoid dry places. Their nest has a most effective air-conditioning system.

A single colony of Macrotermes can number as many as one to three million insects. In one species the queen measures 17.5 cm (7 in) in

world. It moves about in groups except in the breeding season. Then each male establishes a territory where he is joined by one, two, three or more females. The nest is in a hollow in the ground and may reach 3 m (10 ft) in diameter. Each female lays one egg there every other day (a maximum of eight). A total of fifteen to sixty eggs are incubated by the male during the night and by the female during the day. The ostrich egg is on average 15 cm (6 in) long and 13 cm (5 in) wide and weighs up to 1,200 gm (42 oz). Its shell reaches a thickness of 2 mm ($\frac{1}{16}$ in).

Deciduous Forests

From a distance a forest looks like a green wall rising up on the edge of surrounding fields and meadows. As soon as you set foot inside, your view is limited to about 30 or 40 m (100–130 ft). You find also that the air is fresher and calmer than outside.

A forest is the result of many trees growing up together, but other smaller plants and a lot of animals live there too. A tree is a large plant, usually more than 7 m (23 ft) high when fully grown. Its stem consists mostly of wood and is bare of branches up to a certain height. In contrast, a holly, for example, is not so tall and is a shrubby tree. The broom is a shrub. That

is, it has several stems of varying sizes which branch out separately immediately above the surface of the ground.

Certain trees such as oak, beech, chestnut, hornbeam and lime shed their leaves in autumn. They are said to be deciduous. Other trees such as pine, fir and spruce have little stiff, narrow leaves called needles which fall a few at a time all the year round. These trees are called evergreens. They are also known as conifers, because the fruit they bear are in the form of cones.

Trees supply us with timber, resin and cork, among other things. In the mountains they protect the ground against avalanches, and wherever they are, they purify the air and retain a large quantity of water when it rains. This

Moss-covered stump of a tree on which toadstools and bracket fungi are growing.

helps to reduce the incidence of bad flooding caused by the run-off of rain water.

Forests differ according to what man is using them for. A forest is land under cultivation, like a field of corn, the difference being that we have to wait a long time before we can harvest its produce: 20 to 25 years for a copse, 100 to 200 years for a wood, opposed to 5 to 9 months for a field of corn.

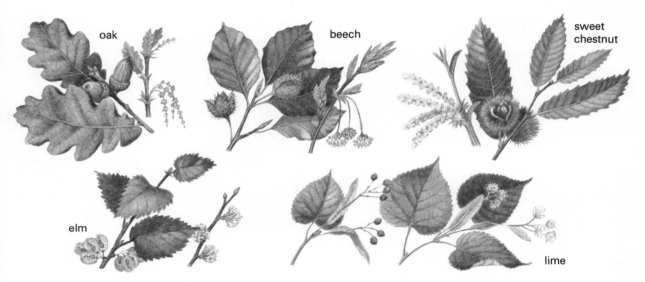

In a copse the trees are cut down and the young shoots are allowed to grow from the base. So all are young and of the same age. When a chestnut or a hornbeam is cut down, the roots remain in the ground and the base of the trunk, the tree stump, is left on the surface. Shoots grow out from the sides of the stump and form a clump or coppice. Many clumps go to make up a copse, which is usually about 10 m (33 ft) high. Its trees are again cut down before they become too big.

Germinating acorns may form little oaks which, growing in a cluster, form first a thicket and later a forest – that is, a collection of trees grown from seed which we leave alone until they become very big. The same result would be achieved if one were to plant seedling oaks and tend them as they grew.

In forests on the plains several different kinds of oak are to be found, such as the sessile, pedunculate and Turkey oaks.

The beech is a common tree which has male flowers that look like little hanging bouquets. The female flowers produce fruits, called beechnuts or mast, two or three coming from each flower. The brown, triangular nuts are each enclosed in a case covered with soft spines. The case opens as it falls to the ground.

The sweet or Spanish chestnut is spread over a large area of southern Europe. Its male flowers, grouped together in long, bright yellow catkins, can be seen at the end of June.

spangle galls

The Temperate Forests of Europe

Flowers are most numerous in forests at the beginning of spring. Later, from June onwards, there are fewer to be seen, for the trees by then have grown all their leaves so that the undergrowth is heavily shaded and receives too little light to grow properly.

From March until May many species flower in quick succession. One of the first, the periwinkle, grows in clumps which cover wide areas. Unlike most of the small or low-growing forest plants the periwinkle keeps its green leaves all year. Its single mauve flowers grow at the very ends of the straight stems. The other stems are creepers.

In March and April the wood anemone, a very common flower, opens its buds. The flowers are white with pink on the outside. Anemones form a thick carpet beneath the oak trees. The flower's corolla closes at night and the 'petals' unfold when the sun has warmed the air. The wood anemone is a perennial, which means that each plant lives for several years (trees are also perennials).

In May Solomon's-seal and lily of the valley flower in the forests. Solomon's-seal has a rhizome or main subterranean stem. At the end

of this there grows each year an aerial stem on which the leaves unfold. The white flowers, which are single or in twos, look like elongated bells. The deep-blue poisonous berries appear in August.

The lily of the valley is known for its perfume. It is also thought to bring good luck. After it has flowered, in August, its leaves become yellow and its bright red berries ripen. They are poisonous too, like the other parts of the plant.

There are other smaller species of trees growing beneath the big ones. The most

ivy

holly

common are the hornbeam and the hazel. The hornbeam has oval leaves like beech leaves, but they are toothed and crinkled. It flowers in the spring before the leaves come out. The hazel flowers very early. Its male flowers, which begin to form into catkins in August, spread their pollen in February. The female flowers look like little red leaves on the ends of buds. The hazel gives shelter and food to several kinds of animal. The hard shell in which its nuts are encased is no obstacle to animals that like to eat the contents.

The dormouse, a pretty little rodent with reddish fur and a hairy tail, feeds on hazelnuts in the autumn before it goes into hibernation, that is, into a deep sleep for the winter.

The nuthatch, a small bird, picks up a nut in its beak and squeezes it into a crack in the bark of a tree. Then it hits the nut again and again with its beak until the shell breaks. The empty shells are left on the tree trunk.

A tiny beetle called the nut-weevil also takes advantage of the fruits of the hazel tree. They provide it with a nesting place and food supplies

elm

birch

maple

hazel dormouse

hazel

nuthatch

for its larvae. Its jaws form a proboscis on which the antennae are hinged at right angles. In May the female pierces the very young nuts with this proboscis and lays an egg in each one. The larva which hatches out eats the kernel of the nut. In autumn the larva cuts a little round hole in the shell, comes out and buries itself in the earth. There it changes into a pupa. The adult does not come out of the pupa until the following spring.

The sycamore is found only in ones or twos in the forest. Its fruits have two little wings which act like propellers as they fall.

Ivy is a climbing plant. It has very long trails which crawl along the ground or hook on to a tree trunk and climb up it by means of densely growing tendrils or clinging roots. The leaves of the ivy stay green all year. When the ivy is old, its straight branches bear leaves that are less indented, almost oval. Flowers appear in September or October. At this time of year its flowers attract honey-gathering insects which the birds come and catch. The fruits of the ivy are not poisonous. First green, then a

deep violet, they ripen at the end of winter, when the blackbirds and jays make the most of them.

The fruit of the holly is not dangerous either. Holly is easily recognized by its stiff leaves which have very sharp points. They stay green all year round.

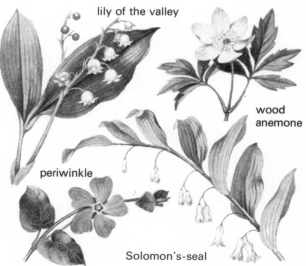

lily of the valley

wood anemone

periwinkle

Solomon's-seal

Plants without Seeds

At the beginning of summer a very different sort of plant starts to appear in the forests. In the undergrowth of coniferous and deciduous forests these plants now grow in increasing numbers. They have neither leaves nor roots, neither stems nor flowers; they reproduce by spores, not by seeds. These special plants are called toadstools. They are a kind of fungus, and they vary greatly in colour and shape.

The name 'toadstool' is applied to the reproductive part of the plant, the rest of which grows among dead leaves, in the earth, forming a network of white threads called a 'mycelium'.

The toadstool itself grows very quickly. If the weather is warm and there is enough moisture in the ground, it pushes up out of the soil and grows to full size in one or two days. After a few days or weeks it disappears, eaten by insects, slugs or small mammals, or simply by rotting away. However, the part which remains beneath ground can live for several years or even as long as a few decades.

These plants have no green pigment, or chlorophyll. This is the substance which gives the green colour to the leaves and stems of most grasses, flowers and trees, and which allows them to make their food with the help of the sun. Because they have no chlorophyll, toadstools are unable to make their own food. They have to live on decomposing matter such as leaves and branches which cover the ground like a thick carpet.

There are a number of common species in European woods which can be eaten as long as they are cooked. The chanterelle appears in July. It sometimes grows in circles called 'fairy rings'. This curious formation comes about because the mycelium underground grows out in all directions from a central point and forms reproductive organs at a certain distance from this point, and nowhere else.

One of the most sought-after edible toadstools is the cep. It sometimes grows so big that its cap measures 25 cm (10 in) in diameter. It grows under oak and sweet chestnut trees.

Mosses often cover large areas at the edges of forest tracks or on open patches where trees

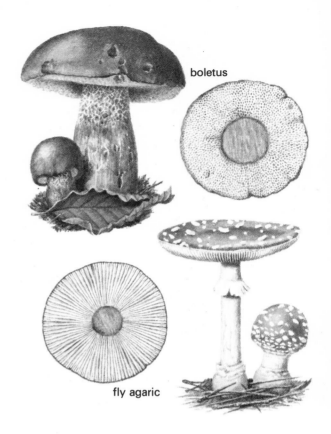

boletus

fly agaric

Toadstools, ferns and mosses growing amidst the undergrowth and fallen leaves.

chantarelle

have been cut down. Some grow on tree trunks, while others form a soft, velvety bed between 10 and 20 cm (4–8 in) thick. Moss is made up of a mass of small green plants, each with a stem and small leaves, but with no real roots. Like mushrooms, they reproduce by means of spores. These are enclosed in little reddish sacs situated at the ends of very thin stems.

Lichens are 'pioneer' plants which succeed in settling on rocks where they attack the surface of the stone. In the little hollows in the surface of the rock there is a gradual accumulation of water and plant waste-matter, such as leaves blown by the wind. Thus a thin bed of humus is built up, making the perfect place for mosses to grow. Most mosses can only grow where the air is very pure. If mosses are growing some-where in abundance, then you can be sure that there is very little, if any, pollution of the atmosphere in that region.

Ferns have roots, leaves (called fronds) and, in their stems, canals in which sap circulates. But they do not have any flowers. On the under-surfaces of the leaves of the polypod can be seen little flat, round sacs containing spores. In contrast to mosses, which stay green all year, several species of fern dry out in autumn. However, their root-stock stays alive.

parasol mushroom

horn of plenty

dung beetle

brimstone
butterfly

Insects of the Temperate Forests of Europe

The male brimstone butterfly has pretty yellow wings with an orange spot, and flies about at the edge of woods from March onwards. It spends the winter hidden under dead leaves and comes out as soon as the sun begins to warm the air. The caterpillar of this species is green with whitish stripes. It feeds on elder and buckthorn leaves. The female brimstone butterfly is a pale yellowish-green.

Other beautiful butterflies can be seen fluttering in the woods, but many are so small that they are difficult to identify, especially as they have few distinguishing characteristics.

Many are classified as pests because their caterpillars attack the leaves of trees.

In deciduous forests, the one moth whose presence is soon noticed is the green tortrix, on oak trees. For five to seven days in June or July it flies around in the treetops. Before she dies, the female lays her eggs two at a time on the twigs of an oak tree at the base of the leaves. They stay there for the whole of the summer, autumn and winter, and at the end of April or the beginning of May, little green caterpillars emerge. They immediately begin to eat the young leaves which are still curled up inside their buds. As the rest of the leaves unfold, the caterpillars eat them right down to the veins, and oak trees which should have been green look a greyish colour from a distance. At the end of May the caterpillars stop causing damage

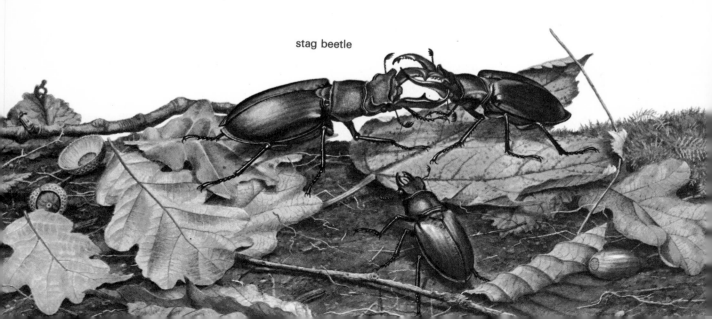

stag beetle

tortrix moth

the ground, about 15 cm (6 in) deep, complete with side tunnels which it fills with dung. In each of these side tunnels it lays an egg. The larvae hatching from the eggs then have food to live on. They spend the winter in the ground, then the following year they metamorphose into pupae, and the perfect insects emerge in June or July.

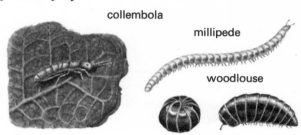

collembola

millipede

woodlouse

and change into chrysalises. Many of these caterpillars together make quite a noise. This is caused by their little black pellets of excrement falling constantly on the dead leaves. You can sometimes see these caterpillars hanging from silk threads attached to the foliage of the tree.

The green tortrix is a prey of many insects. Wasps lay their eggs in the bodies of the caterpillars, which provide the larvae with food when they hatch. At least forty species of birds eat the moth and its caterpillars, but when the green tortrix begins to multiply, they cannot destroy all of them. The moths reproduce regularly in fact. Oak trees which have been attacked by the caterpillars are able to replace the foliage that has been destroyed, but the amount of wood they can produce is less than usual. This, then, is a very good example of little creatures having an extremely damaging effect when there are enough of them.

Large insects seem rare in the forest because they spend the greater part of their life in the form of larvae hidden in wood or bark. One of the largest is the stag beetle. The males have very long, branched mandibles, looking like antlers. This beetle feeds on sap and emerges at the end of June or in July, particularly at nightfall. The larva spends five or six years in tunnels that it makes inside the trunk of an old oak tree.

The dung beetle, one of the most common forest beetles, feeds on the droppings of mammals. In July it makes a vertical shaft in

Shredded by insects and other little animals and softened by rain, the dead leaves which carpet the forest floor turn into a blackish substance called humus in about two to three years. This leaf-mould, as it is often called, gradually merges with the earth beneath and contains many elements vital for sustaining plant life.

A black beetle called the leaf-roller deposits its eggs inside rolled-up leaves. The female cuts an S-shape in each half of the leaf blade and pulls the pieces away from each cut. She then rolls them one on top of the other and lays two to five eggs inside the tube. It takes her only an hour to complete this complicated work. The larvae stay in their cradle for two to three months, after which time they emerge, fall to the ground and change into pupae.

birch leaf-roller

Birds of the Temperate Forests of Europe

robin redbreast

Winter is by far the best season to see forest birds because there are no leaves on the trees to hide them. With the exception of the green woodpecker, the woodpeckers spend their whole lives climbing up and down trees, exploring the bark and hollowing out the wood which has been attacked by insect larvae. When they stop to eat, they hang on with their claws and rest their weight on their tail, which has very stiff feathers. They make a nest in a tree, drilling a hole by chipping away thousands of

greater spotted woodpecker

claw

green woodpecker

little pieces of wood and bark. The nest has an opening to the outside through a round hole, 5–6 cm (2–2½ in) across in the case of the greater spotted woodpecker. The nest is sunk about 20 or 30 cm (8–12 in) into the tree. At the bottom the woodpecker leaves some soft chippings on which four to six white eggs are laid. The greater spotted woodpecker does not

sing. It has a sharp cry, but at the end of the winter it can sometimes be heard making a curious drumming sound. The bird chooses a dead tree and strikes the wood with its beak many times in quick succession (twelve to fourteen times per second at least).

The robin redbreast lives in the forest, but it is also found in parks and gardens where there are bushes. The young have a brown and beige plumage, different from that of their parents. The redbreast rarely lives longer than three years. It is often a prey to sparrowhawks or weasels, small carnivorous mammals, and its nest is often destroyed even though it is carefully hidden.

The song thrush builds her nest in hedges among the branches of a hazel or other shrub, between shoots growing out of the trunk of a big oak tree, or among ivy. The nest is cup-

nest of song thrush

shaped, made of a thick layer of grasses and roots, sometimes with moss, leaves and twigs, and lined with a smooth coating of rotten wood and dung mixed with saliva.

The brown or tawny owl is one of the most common nocturnal birds in the forests of temperate Europe. Its big black eyes are sensitive to the slightest light and enable it to hunt in what seems to our eyes total darkness. Its eyes are situated on the front of the head. The owl also has very acute hearing, and it is by picking up the noises of its small prey that the bird can locate them. The owl hunts many different kinds of animal, including blackbirds, finches, fieldmice, shrews, earthworms, frogs

tawny owl

jay's feather

and insects. It is silent in flight for its wings have soft, downy feathers. During the day it sleeps, hidden amongst the foliage or perched on a branch against the trunk of a large tree.

The buzzard makes its nest in the branches of a very large tree. In April the female lays two or three eggs which are white with brown markings. The eggs are incubated by the female for about thirty-four days. When they hatch, the young are covered in white down and already have their eyes open. They gradually grow brown feathers. The adult birds bring

them moles, fieldmice and young blackbirds, but especially rabbits.

For a long time the buzzard was killed because it ate wild rabbits. In fact, it was not responsible for the drop in the rabbit population; it was man who nearly exterminated this little mammal by spreading a disease called myxomatosis, about twenty years ago.

The buzzard glides like an aeroplane on its wide wings. In February and March it can be seen circling high in the sky. It drops suddenly, then soars up again to repeat its trick.

buzzard

Mammals of the Temperate Forests of Europe

roe deer   roe buck

Animals which feed their young with milk produced by special glands called mammary glands are known as mammals. Several species of different sizes live in the forest. The red deer is one of the largest. There is a clear difference in size between the male, or stag, and the smaller female, or hind. Until the age of three months, the young are called calves. They are easily recognized by their spotted coats. Only the males have antlers. These are rather like bare bones which begin to grow at the age of one year. While the horns of cows and goats are permanent, the antlers of a red deer are shed

regularly in March and start growing again not long after. While they are growing, they are covered with a fine coat of soft hair called 'velvet'. Until the deer is twelve or thirteen years old, the antlers grow bigger each time they are renewed and become more and more branched every year.

It is very difficult to see a deer during the day, unless it is disturbed. In the evenings it comes out of hiding to eat grass, young shoots, leaves and in autumn acorns and beechnuts. Most of the year, the adult males live alone while the hinds stay with the calves and young deer in small groups. But in October the males, or stags, come back to the hinds in order to mate with them. At this time of year, they appear to be very touchy – they bellow (this is called belling) and sometimes the stags fight with their antlers.

The roe deer is a much smaller animal, living in woods with thin cover, surrounded by meadows and fields. It comes out of the forest

red deer stag

red deer hinds

more often than other deer. It also likes plantations and clearings, places where the vegetation is low-lying. The young males, or yearlings, also called brockets, have small antlers without any branches. These are shed in November, but have grown again completely by April or May. In the mating season – August – the male, or buck, does not leave the female, or doe, and they follow each other around bushes and meadows so much that they make small circular tracks, known as roe-rings, in the grass.

The roe deer chooses its food carefully, munching here and there on shoots and young stems. After a feed it rests so that it can ruminate. This means that it chews the food it has rapidly swallowed while grazing or browsing and which has already gone through the first stages of digestion in the rumen, a big pouch in its stomach. When a roe deer is disturbed it barks and looks up to see what is happening, then bounds away. It is then that

dormouse

an observer will see the two big spots of white hair on his hindquarters.

The dormouse has the reputation of being a long sleeper. It falls into a deep sleep in the autumn and does not wake again until May. It spends the winter in a hollow tree or in a hole in the ground where it makes a nest out of moss and dry grasses. While it is asleep, its breathing and heart-beat slow right down.

hedgehog

shrew

badger

Red deer stag roars a challenge to his rival as he rounds up the hinds for the breeding season.

59

Coniferous Forests

The trees in coniferous forests stay green all year. There is however, one exception. This is the larch, which sheds its leaves in autumn, like the broad-leaved trees. The larch grows high up on the mountains, but it has been planted widely in Britain and North America both as an ornamental tree and for its wood.

Coniferous trees have small, narrow leaves called 'needles'. Such trees are called evergreens. Inside the trunk and the branches are channels filled with an aromatic liquid called resin. Most conifers grow naturally only in the

Mountain ash flower and its fruit, known as the rowanberry, is sometimes found in conifer plantations.

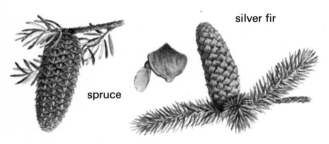

mountains. But man has planted several different species on the plains, such as the Scots pine, the black pine, the larch and the spruce.

The silver fir forms magnificent forests on Europe's main mountain ranges. It has a conical shape when young. As it grows older, its top flattens out and is recognizably different from the top of the spruce which remains pointed all its life. The needles of this fir have rounded, slightly grooved ends. There are two

white resinous lines running parallel on their lower surface which give the tree its name. The cones, which stand up straight on the branches, can be distinguished from the spruce cones as the latter hang down.

The spruce grows wild throughout Europe and is planted widely in Britain for timber. It is also used in North America, as an ornamental tree, because it can grow in almost any soil. Its roots do not go down very deep and it is apt to be blown down in gales. The tree casts a great deal of shade. In a plantation of twenty or thirty-year-old spruce trees you will not find any other plants, because the ground is covered by a thick blanket of needles, which are also very stiff and grouped together in pairs. These trees need a lot of light, but they will grow in almost any soil, even sand. It is quite common to see bracken growing in forests of Scots pine and maritime pine, as well as in forests of chestnut and birch.

pines

bracken

Roe deer on the edge of a plantation of young fir trees in northern Europe.

Insects of Coniferous Forests

Living in coniferous forests are colonies of ants which hollow out nests inside tree trunks. They are generally hidden from view, except when the black woodpecker drills holes in the wood in order to reach them. With their strong jaws, these ants gnaw through the new rings of soft

carpenter ant

wood formed during spring growth.

Much more abundant and more easily seen are the red wood ants which move around during the daytime. If you follow these insects, you will end up either at a tree which they climb up or at a mound of vegetable rubbish,

especially pine needles. This is the ants' nest, which can sometimes be more than 1 m (3 ft) high. The red ant is a social insect that lives in very large colonies, varying in numbers from 100,000 to 1 million insects. The population consists mostly of workers, which are sterile females, that is, females unable to breed, a few males and a queen (or up to a hundred) which lays from 10 to 300 eggs each day for the six months of the breeding season.

The workers hunt other insects, gather the

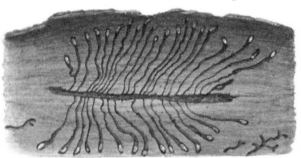

tunnels of engraver beetle

sweet droppings of greenfly or stay in the nest to guard it, keep clear the passages inside, and to look after the eggs, the larvae and the pupae, which are commonly called 'ants' eggs'. It has been estimated that every day in the summer, a really large colony of wood ants destroys about

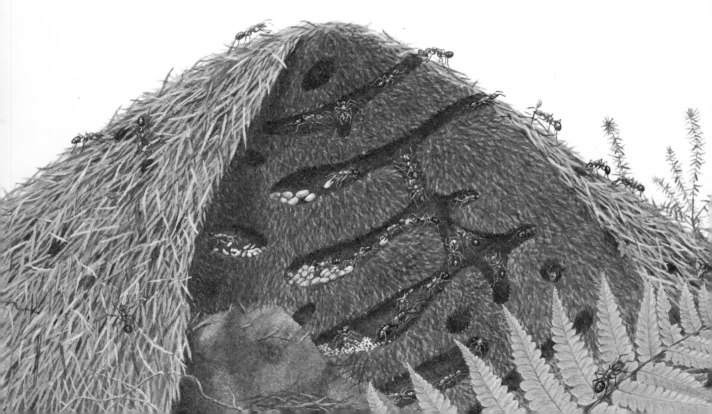

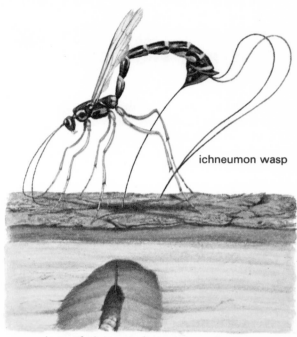

ichneumon wasp

larva of giant wood wasp

100,000 insects, 40% of which are noxious, that is, troublesome to crops. The workers live for two to three years, but the queen may live for fifteen or twenty years.

There are two varieties of wasp that war with each other in the forest. The first, called the giant wood wasp lays its eggs in the trunk of a pine or spruce. The female has an egg-laying organ called an ovipositor which she forces into the hard wood (it takes her a quarter of an hour at least, sometimes two hours, to do this). She lays several eggs in each hole, and goes on drilling until she has laid between 300 and 500 eggs. As the larvae grow, they make bigger and bigger passages inside the wood, but before changing into pupae, they are often attacked by the parasitic rhyssa wasp, which is also known as an ichneumon fly.

The female rhyssa wasp has an extremely long ovipositor nearly twice her own length. She stands firmly on her six legs and inserts the ovipositor into the wood, then she lays an egg in the larva of a giant wood wasp. But how does she manage to locate the larva? She is probably guided by her sense of smell, but there are other signs which help her. Often, however, she is wasting her time, as when she is unable to locate a larva. It may take the rhyssa wasp as little as twenty minutes to drill through several thicknesses of healthy wood.

Anthill of the European red ant cut across to show some of the tunnels inside where eggs, larvae and pupae are stored.

Mammals and Birds of Mixed Woodlands

fox

The wild boar gives the impression of being a formidable creature. It is big, and it also moves very fast. Yet the only time it is dangerous is when it is wounded, is being pursued or has been suddenly disturbed without warning.

The wild boar belongs to a family of hoofed mammals, the Suidae. It is ancestor to the domestic pig or hog. The male, or boar, has long canine teeth in the lower jaw. These stick out of its mouth and the boar uses them to defend itself. The newly-born wild boar, or piglet, has a striped coat. The mother is known

wild boar sow

wild boar piglets

as a sow. The adult male lives alone and the only time he goes near the female is for the purpose of mating. The wild boar lives in, and on the edge of, forests, by ponds and in thickets. It has a varied diet and will eat almost anything animal or vegetable. An animal that eats a wide variety of animal and plant foods is said to be omnivorous.

The fox is carnivorous and eats only meat. It

has the reputation of being a very cunning animal, perhaps because it has a sly look but also because it is clever at stealing chickens and at avoiding capture. The fox, the most common of the medium-sized mammals in the Northern Hemisphere, lives in woods, in thickets and on the edges of forests, sometimes not far from houses. It is rarely seen during the day, except in undisturbed areas. Its earth, which is the place where it sleeps, has an opening of about 30 cm (12 in) in diameter. If the earth is occupied, there are no spiders' webs across the entrance, and tracks can be seen leading inside.

Since 1968 foxes in Europe have been affected by a deadly disease called rabies, which is contagious and can be spread to other mammals and to birds.

Of all the mammals living in the forest, the easiest to pick out is the red squirrel. Like the pine marten and the fat dormouse it spends

red squirrel

field vole

most of its life in the trees. Its colour varies from red to brown and even black, but whatever its colour it is generally darker in winter. It is very active during the day, and feeds on new shoots, buds, toadstools, hazelnuts, beechmast, acorns and pine seeds. At the foot of spruce trees, where squirrels like to eat sometimes, one can often find peeled cones, surrounded by the scales which the squirrels have pulled off with their teeth to uncover the little seeds inside. The squirrel sleeps at the top of a tree in a nest made of small branches, dry leaves, moss, bark and fibres. In this comfortable nest are born between five and seven babies in April or May.

The coal-tit is one of the most typical perching birds in pine and spruce forests. The crossbill never leaves the conifer forests because they provide it with the only food it likes – the seeds of pines which it extracts very easily with its crossed bill. The crossbill lives in the mountains, but some years it is possible to see members of the species on the plains. Crossbills are birds that have been driven out of their natural habitat by lack of food.

The hazel dormouse is a very small animal. It makes a nest for itself from moss and dry grass, placing it a little way up in a bush on the edge of an evergreen forest. It has a passion for hazelnuts. It spends the winter in hibernation, lying still, as if dead, in a nest under the dead leaves covering the ground.

The marten or pine marten catches rodents and birds such as the young black woodpecker which it pulls out of its nest-hole in a tree. It is one of the few predators of the biggest woodpecker in Europe.

Above: Pine marten dragging a black woodpecker from its nest in a hole in a tree.

great tit

crossbill

woodcock

65

Bonelli's eagle

The Mediterranean Shrubland and Heath

There is a special scrub in the Mediterranean region known as the maquis. The vegetation there is very thick and reaches a height of 2 to 3 m (6–10 ft) or more. On the other hand, plants in heathland are hardly ever more than 50 cm to 1 m (20 in–3 ft) high and grow in tufts with open space between. In these two areas of countryside there are plants and animals which cannot be found anywhere else.

chermes oak

cork oak

This is true of the chermes oak, the olive and lavender.

The chermes oak is small and has spiny, holly-like leaves and acorns that take two years to ripen.

The olive is very sensitive to frost. Although wild olives grow in the valley of the Rhône in France, a cultivated variety arose in Greece. This is also grown as a crop in Portugal and California. Lavender grows in big bushes on stony ground. On the ends of its stems are long, thin violet-coloured flower heads with a lovely perfume. Many flies and bees come buzzing around in search of pollen and nectar.

A large black and yellow insect related to the greenfly lives in the Mediterranean region. It is the cicada, which most people know better as a tropical insect. Its mouth has a sort of stiff beak, or proboscis, which it pushes into the twigs of shrubs to suck up the sap. It lays eggs from

lizard

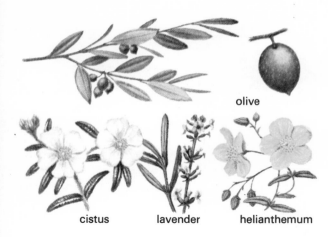

olive

cistus   lavender   helianthemum

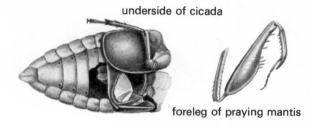

underside of cicada

foreleg of praying mantis

which hatch larvae looking exactly like miniature adults.

The larva lives underground for four years, changing its skin several times before it finally becomes an adult insect. In the United States lives the seventeen-year-locust. It is not a locust but a cicada which spends seventeen years as a larva. Male cicadas have a device in their abdomen for producing a loud, repetitive sound like a song or a chant. This consists of two shell-like drums vibrated by strong muscles.

The praying mantis is also found in the Mediterranean region as well as in tropical countries. In the United States praying mantises are sometimes called devil's coach horses or mule killers. The praying mantis is so named because it raises the forepart of its body and holds its long, barbed legs in front of it like somebody praying. It sits very still in the grass, waiting for an insect such as a fly or a cricket to come near. It cannot be seen because it is camouflaged by its green or brown colour. When an insect does go by within its reach, the praying mantis throws out its front legs, and devours it.

The praying mantis is not just carnivorous; it is also cannibalistic, for the female sometimes eats the male during mating! The male · is smaller than the female.

The green lizard is one of the biggest European lizards. It has very small teeth which it uses to grasp and chew prey, such as insects and spiders. In May the female lays six to ten eggs at the bottom of a hole in the ground. The eggs are very large – about 16 mm ($\frac{5}{8}$ in) long – almost oval-shaped and have a soft, shell-like, fine skin. Inside, the little lizard develops and

it hatches out after sixty to ninety days.

Bonelli's eagle hunts rabbits, jackdaws and rats. This bird of prey, now very rare, finds a place for its nest in a niche in a wall of rock.

Several types of warbler live in the scrub and heathland. They all eat insects, and for this reason most of them fly south in the autumn because their prey have disappeared. The Sardinian warbler is similar to the more widespread blackcap, from which it differs mainly

European wild rabbit

droppings

in its smaller size, its black hood, which comes right down to its eyes, and its song, which is less tuneful. Warblers make their little nest from dry grasses. Like most birds they use it for only one sitting or during only one spring. The nest is not very solid, and falls apart in winter, so each year the birds have to build another one. They never use their nest as a dwelling; it is purely and simply a cradle for the eggs and the young.

The wild rabbit is another heath-dweller. It is found almost everywhere else as well, but its numbers are greater in some areas than others.

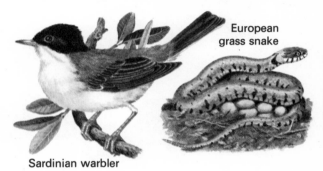

European grass snake

Sardinian warbler

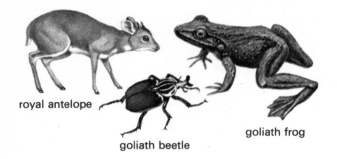

royal antelope

goliath beetle

goliath frog

gaboon viper

African pitta

African Rain Forests

Rain forests are so called because they have a very high rainfall – at least 1.5 to 2 m (60–80 in) of rain per year, and as much as 6 m (235 in). The animals and plants, having such an ideal environment, are prolific. There are 700 species of tree in the Cameroun rain forests and in an area of 2 hectares (5 acres) in Malaysia 200 species have been counted; in temperate regions the number is nearer a dozen. In Ceylon there are 1,500 species and in the Amazon about 2,500. There is also an astonishing number of species of animals.

In Colombia, in South America, for example, there are 1,550 species of bird (as against 480 in the whole of Europe) 200 species of amphibian,

350 species of reptile, more than 300 species of mammal and 1,000 freshwater fishes.

The Amazon is the home of more than 100,000 plant and animal species. The dampness and warmth – an average of 25°C (77°F) – are good conditions for large cold-blooded animals. But there are relatively few members of each species, and large groups of big mammals are not found together as they are on the savannah. The vegetation is always green and lush. Although the rain forests do not boast the biggest trees in the world (the giant sequoias live in North America and eucalyptus in temperate Australia), there are trees which reach a height of 70 m (230 ft) and tower above the canopy formed at 30 or 40 m (100–130 ft) by the rest of the trees. Creepers climb up the tree trunks, while orchids and other plants called

gorilla

bushpig

okapi

harnessed antelope

leopard

68

Diana monkey

epiphytes, grow on the trees but are not parasitic. They push their roots into the decaying plant matter which accumulates in the forks of branches.

The undergrowth is bright and the layer of dead leaves is very thin as the leaves decompose very quickly. Fifty years ago the rain forests formed a band across America, Africa and Asia, but satellite photographs have shown that they are now reduced to isolated areas – man is destroying them. Large areas do exist however in the basins of the Amazon and the Congo, in Gabon, in Borneo, in New Guinea

and here and there throughout South-East Asia.

In Africa there are not many big mammals living in this environment. One of them is the forest elephant, a sub-species of the bush elephant, which grows no taller at the shoulder than 1.95 m (6 ft). Another is the dwarf buffalo. In Liberia there is a pygmy hippo-potamus that lives in the forest pools. The okapi is a close relative of the giraffe and was not discovered until 1900 in Zaire. The stripes on its coat act as a camouflage in the dark forest where the rays of light filter through. The royal antelope, the smallest antelope in the world, only 25 cm (10 in) high, never leaves the rain forest. It is scarcely heavier than the goliath frog which has a maximum weight of nearly 3.6 kg (8 lb).

The Gaboon viper, the largest puff adder, is equipped with unusually long venomous fangs.

69

gibbon

Asian Jungles

In contrast to the African lion, the tiger is one of the animals that is threatened with extinction because it has been hunted for its skin. It is the only big cat that has earned the reputation of being a man-eater. Yet the number of victims is low – about a hundred per year over the last ten years – and in most cases tigers have attacked because they have been disturbed. The

magnificent feline seldom climbs trees, but it swims well and in a single bound can cover a distance of 6 to 7 m (20–23 ft) and a height of 2 to 3 m (6–10 ft). It can creep along unseen in grass 60 to 70 cm (24–28 in) high. The tigress gives birth to usually three or four babies, called cubs, which are blind at birth and weigh from 1 to 1.5 kg (2–3 lb). The cubs are often killed by bears or other carnivores. Occasionally a tiger dies as the result of an encounter with a porcupine. This animal has quills 20 cm (8 in)

python

tarsier

swampy forests to the south of western Bengal seem to be the only areas where the tiger still frequently attacks man, simply because they come in contact with him more often. The tiger still survives in India, Indonesia, Malaysia (Sumatra), China and in Russia in the province of Ussuri, bordering Manchuria, where there are less than a hundred left now. It is in this part of Siberia that the biggest tigers live.

The tiger attacks all kinds of prey, not only large animals. Its diet consists mainly of deer, antelopes, gaurs (wild cattle) and wild pigs, but it also captures birds, lizards, turtles, fish, frogs and crabs, even grasshoppers; and it eats some fruit. It has been estimated that in one year a tiger will kill at least thirty large animals each weighing about 100 kg (220 lb). Its uncommon strength exceeds even that of a lion. This

or more long and as thick as pencils, and these slowly work into the tiger's body and penetrate the internal organs.

The biggest snakes in the world are the anaconda of South America and the reticulated python of South-East Asia and the Sunda Isles. The python reaches a length of 10 m (33 ft) and a weight of over 100 kg (220 lb). It is said, although not proven, that bigger specimens have been killed. The reticulated python is one of the constrictor snakes.

Indian or Asiatic elephant

fruit pigeon

male bird-of-paradise

cassowary

Below: A tiger creeping through the long grass sees a barking deer. Soon it will crouch for the final spring to seize the deer.

South American Rain Forests

It is often thought that the rain forests of tropical America are inhabited by many brightly coloured humming birds, but in fact the most brilliantly coloured species are visitors of gardens, orchards and wooded grasslands. Forest species have a relatively sombre plumage to tone in with the deep shadows. Some hummingbirds are tiny: the largest weighs only 20 g ($\frac{3}{4}$ oz); the smallest do not weigh more than 2 g ($\frac{1}{16}$ oz) when fully grown. The total length varies from 5 to 21 cm (2–8 in) according to the species, of which half is accounted for by the beak and tail. These cheeky birds live only in America, from Alaska to Tierra del Fuego but the greatest number of species (a total of 163 out of 237) are found in regions close to the Equator. They inhabit different types of country, and some live as high as 5,000 m (16,000 ft) in the Andes Mountains. The heart of these little birds beats 500 to 1,200 times per minute, according to whether they are resting or flying. Their wings move so quickly back and forth that they make a humming sound. Hummingbirds can, like some insects, fly forward, backward, or sideways, or hover in the same spot like a helicopter. Some make an elaborate nest which protects their two white eggs and their chicks from damp and cold. The female alone makes the nest, incubates the eggs

hummingbirds

male quetzal

female quetzal

blue-and-yellow macaw

toucan

Brazilian tapir

agouti

jaguar

and feeds the babies. The smallest eggs measure 9 by 6 mm ($\frac{1}{4} \times \frac{3}{8}$ in). Hummingbirds eat the nectar of flowers and insects hidden in their corollas.

The macaw, belonging to the parrot family, is found from southern Mexico to Ecuador, in Bolivia, Brazil and in the north of Paraguay. It lays two to four white eggs in a hole in a tree.

Toucans live only in tropical America. These strange-looking birds have an enormous beak, sometimes as big as their body, and splashed with bright colours, but we still do not know what this huge bill is actually used for. It may be used in mating displays, or for taking hold of fruit.

tamarins

two-toed sloth

The quetzal is one of the most beautiful birds of Central America, but it is becoming more and more rare as the mountain forests are exploited. The males have a train of tail coverts measuring up to 60 cm (2 ft) in length. These feathers are not moulted after reaching their full size when the bird is four years old. The quetzal is the national emblem of Guatemala. This bird nests in holes in old, rotten tree trunks, enlarging them with its beak.

Some strange mammals spend nearly all their lives in the trees of the forest. They are the seven species of sloth. The forefeet of these animals have either two or three claws and the hindfeet always have three toes no matter what the species. They spend much of their time hanging upside-down from the branches, with their backs towards the ground. Their thick fur protects them from the rain. Tiny algae grow amongst their hairs and give them a greenish tinge. Tiny moths also live among their hair. Their eggs are laid in the sloth's excrement, the caterpillars grow there, change into pupae and later the moths fly off in search of other sloths. The moths have a close relationship with the mammals, living on the secretion of the sebaceous glands which are found at the bases of the hairs. As their name suggests, sloths are very slow – it takes them six hours to cover 1.5 km (1 mile)!

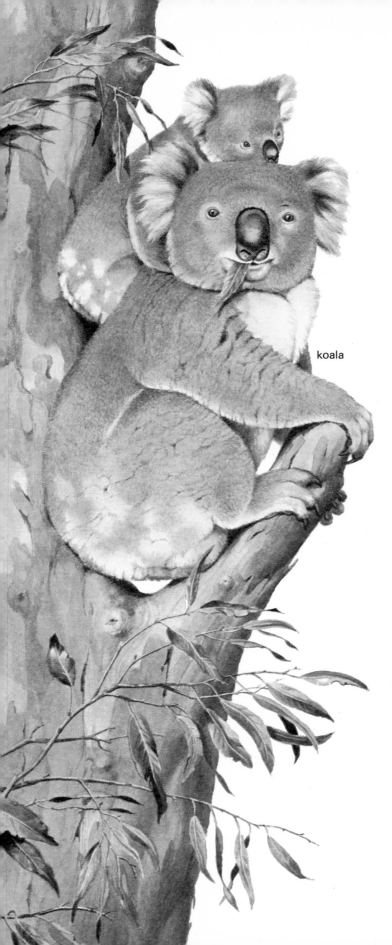

koala

Australasian Forests

In Australia there is a belt of rain forest in the north-east along the coast. Forests in other parts of the country are drier and consist partly of eucalyptus trees. These are of very varied appearance as there are 700 species, some of which are quite small, while others reach a height of 120 m (400 ft). In lightly wooded scrubland or grassland live the big kangaroos, which may be up to 2 m (6 ft) tall. These animals are mammals belonging to the group called marsupials. Marsupials (pouched animals) live only in Australia, Tasmania, New Guinea, on the island of Celebes and in tropical America, extending northwards as far as the southern United States. The red kangaroo moves by leaping on its hindlegs, its tail acting as a balancer. When the kangaroo is still, the tail is like a third leg resting on the ground. Normally, the animal takes bounds of 1.5 m (5 ft) at the most, but when fleeing from an enemy it can cover 6 to 9 m (20–30 ft) in a single leap and it is capable of travelling at 40 km (25 miles) per hour. The young kangaroo is born in embryonic form after a gestation of only 28 to 38 days. It measures only 25 to 30 mm

satin bowerbird

male

female

$(1–1\frac{1}{4}$ in) and weighs about 1.5 g $(\frac{1}{20}$ oz). Once out of its mother's body, it climbs up into her pouch without any help and attaches itself to one of the teats inside. It shows its head for the first time after 150 days and comes out after 190 days, but it does not leave the pouch for good until around 235 days old. Other smaller kangaroos, the wallabies and tree kangaroos, live

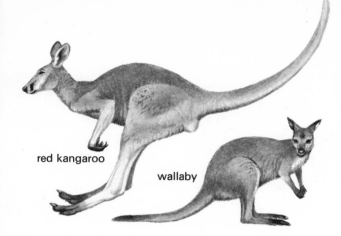

red kangaroo

wallaby

respectively in grassland dotted with bushes, and in forest trees where they move about with great agility.

The koala is one of the best-known marsupials. It is rather like a small furry bear. It is not very active during the day and moves about more at night. It lives mainly on the leaves of the eucalyptus tree. It consumes about 1 kg (2 lb) of these leaves per day.

The koala is an excellent climber because it has long claws on its toes. The female has only one baby at a time. When it is five to six months old, the baby leaves the marsupial pouch and rides on its mother's back. It appears that the koala hardly ever lives longer than twelve or thirteen years, even though it does not have any natural predators.

Bats are a very important group of mammals. More than 900 species are known. They are the only mammals capable of true flight – their front limbs are like wings, the fingers are extremely long and covered by a flight membrane. They are nocturnal and spend the day in some kind of shelter, such as a cave, a hole in a wall or tree, or in a barn. The flying fox of Australia, one of the fruit bats, however, sleeps in the open,

hanging upside-down by its feet from a branch. Fruit bats form noisy colonies of hundreds or even thousands. They feed on fruit and flowers and move about from one region to another as the fruit in different places ripens. The biggest of the fruit-eating flying foxes, the kalong of Malaysia, has a maximum wing span of 1.7 m ($5\frac{1}{2}$ ft).

Australia and New Guinea are the home of two of the most primitive mammals: the duckbill or platypus, which as its name suggests has

echidna

flying phalanger

a bill like a duck, and the echidna or spiny anteater. There are five species of echidna which resemble large hedgehogs. They all lay soft-shelled eggs. The females do not have any teats; the milk simply oozes through slits on her abdomen where it is licked up by the babies.

New Zealand lies 2,000 km (1,250 miles) to the south-east of Australia and has a number of endemic animals – this means that they can be found nowhere else in the world. There are three species of kiwi, which are flightless running birds without wings and with hair-like body feathers. They are nocturnal and they eat mostly worms and insects which they detect by their sense of smell. The female usually lays two large eggs which measure 12 by 7.5 cm ($4\frac{3}{4}$ × 3 in) in the largest species.

flying foxes (fruit bats)

kookaburra

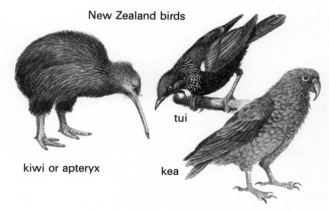

New Zealand birds

tui

kiwi or apteryx

kea

Fresh Waters

The vegetation which grows on the banks of rivers and ponds consists of plants which have adapted to damp ground. Some of them are even able to live underwater for a time when the level of the river or pond rises. This is true of the common alder, which can be recognized by its fan-like, toothed leaves. The flowers are catkins and appear at the end of the winter. The fruits which follow them look a bit like tiny pine-cones. This tree will die if its roots are underwater for a long time, because the roots are unable to breathe.

The willow is a tree which is often prevented from growing tall by regular pruning. This is known as pollarding. A pollarded willow has a strout trunk with a crown of slender branches. As it gets old, its 'heart' (the centre of the trunk) rots and is converted into mould, and only a thin layer of living wood on the inside of the bark is left to keep the tree alive.

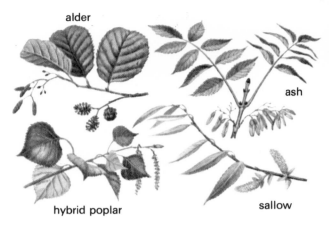

alder

ash

hybrid poplar

sallow

The hybrid poplar is widely cultivated and comes from an American species related to the black poplar. It is often found on the banks of rivers and in other cool, damp places. In poplar plantations the trees are arranged in straight, regularly spaced rows. In the right environment the poplar grows relatively quickly. After thirty years it measures 50 cm (20 in) in diameter and 20 to 25 m (65–80 ft) in height. It is

yellow flag iris

meadow sweet

bur reed

water forget-me-not

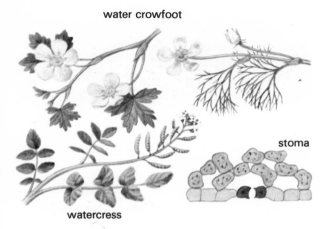

water crowfoot

stoma

watercress

then ready to be cut down. In March one can see the deep red male catkins on its branches which are still without leaves. The young leaves which then burst from the sticky buds are copper-coloured before they turn green.

The ash is a very common tree near fresh water, but it may also be a forest tree. Like the robinia, or false acacia, it has composite leaves, that is, leaves that are formed from several leaflets (little leaves). There are between nine and fifteen of these leaflets, each fixed onto a central axis by a short stem. In the autumn, instead of turning red or yellow, they become covered for most of the time in blackish spots, or they fall while they are still completely green.

Like the leaves of many other plants, the leaves of the ash have on their underside tiny openings called stomata, (stoma means a little mouth; stomata is plural) through which they give off water vapour. This process is called transpiration. It aids the absorption of water by the roots and helps the sap to rise. But the leaves have other functions too; they make the plant's food. They are packed with microscopic particles of chlorophyl, a substance which gives them their green colour. The chorophyl absorbs energy from the sun's rays and makes food-materials for the plant. At the same time the plant gives off oxygen and takes in carbon dioxide. Green plants, therefore, are responsible for supplying oxygen to other living creatures, particularly animals.

water mint

Running Waters

crayfish

There are about 6,000 species of animals, mostly insects, living in the freshwaters of central Europe. Of these, about 3,200 live in the rivers and streams, but there are only about 1,000 species in rapid streams and torrents where the current makes it very difficult for many animal species to survive. The animal life

mayfly

dragonfly larva

salmon parr

salmon

newly hatched salmon

varies, depending on whether the bottom is sandy, stony or muddy. The animals in streams feed on aquatic plants (algae, mosses, flowering plants), on waste from animals or on the dead bodies of other animals.

'Ephemera' is the scientific name given to the insects with big transparent wings which can be seen flying over rivers in spring. They are also known as mayflies. The larvae and the adults have three long filaments at the end of the abdomen. The name 'ephemera' suggests that the adults do not live long, sometimes only for one day! That is, they are ephemeral. This is just enough time for them to reproduce. They eat nothing and they mate at nightfall. The larvae, however, go on growing for one to three years according to the species.

Dragonflies appear in fine weather. They can be seen near freshwater, but some, especially the males, will pursue flies and mosquitoes a long way from water, even into forests. The calopteryx dragonfly stays on the edge of rivers

Two dippers in a mountain stream, one perched on a rock, the other, searching for water insects, is completely submerged beneath the water.

kingfisher

male grey wagtail

fish itself. The crayfish is carnivorous and feeds at night on dead, but not rotten, fish, insect larvae and fish eggs (spawn). While it is growing, the young crayfish sheds its outer covering seven or eight times in one year.

The dipper is an amazing bird. It can dive under the water and seems to be able to walk around on the bottom. In fact, it keeps down by the way it holds its wings not by gripping pebbles with its toes, as used to be thought. It eats between 60 and 80 g (2–3 oz) of food per day.

beaver

otter

and settles on the leaves of lilies or other floating plants. All dragonflies have a very long abdomen and a large head with compound eyes. In the large species each eye may be made up of 10,000 facets. Their larvae live in the water.

The crayfish is the biggest shellfish living in freshwaters in Europe. It is becoming scarce now because man has polluted the streams where it lives. He has also overfished the cray-

Still Waters: Vegetation

The water of streams, torrents and rivers is running fresh water, while that in pools, ponds and lakes is stagnant or still. The only movement in the water of pools, ponds and lakes is caused by the wind.

The chemical composition of the water is of vital importance to the life of plants and aquatic animals. In acid water, both plants and animals are rare and not very varied. Similarly, water that is rich in food but poor in oxygen is ideal for certain algae but unsuitable for other living creatures.

The water of ponds is often invaded by quite a dense form of vegetation called duckweed. This makes a bright green carpet on the surface.

The leaves of each individual plant are tiny – in one of the most common species the oval leaves are only 3 mm ($\frac{1}{8}$ in) across. They are floating plants, but they have tiny roots which extract food from the water. The little yellowish flowers come out in May or June. They serve no purpose in reproduction. The plant reproduces by budding.

Reeds and reed mace dry out and become

yellow waterlily

arrowhead

reeds

reed r

yellow in winter. But the stump that is left produces new shoots each spring so that the plant grows back. Reeds belong to the same family as grasses. In August a tuft of brown flowers blooms at the end of each stem.

The reed mace, sometimes mistakenly called the bulrush, can be easily recognized by the distinctive flowers. The female flowers form a long cylinder 2 or 3 cm ($\frac{3}{4}$–$1\frac{1}{4}$ in) in diameter.

This is topped by the narrower casing of male flowers. The male cylinder drops off very quickly. The female flowers, which are numerous and very tightly packed, become separated by the rain and, at the end of the winter, dispersed by the wind. Each seed has a little parachute which can carry it a great distance. If it falls in the right environment, the seed will germinate.

water caltrops

willow

flowering rush

kingcup

Still Waters: Small Animals

The still waters of ponds are teeming with small creatures. Those most obvious to the naked eye are insects and snails but there are also the many tiny water fleas. The most numerous belong to the group Protozoa, or single-celled animals. These can only be seen with the aid of a magnifying-glass or a microscope.

The paramecium, or slipper animalcule, is a giant among these single-celled animals, reaching a length of 0.2 mm ($\frac{1}{100}$ in)! You may be able to see one if you pour some pond water into a small container. The paramecium was the first of the protozoa to be discovered (in 1675). Its body is covered with between 10,000 and 15,000 'celia', which are like minute hairs. By waving its cilia, a paramecium is able to move forward at a speed of 2 to 2.5 m (6–8 ft) per second when the temperature is about 20°C (68°F). This little animal consists of a single cell. It has no skeleton, no eyes, no heart, no lungs, but it does have a mouth. It swallows bacteria and microscopic plants as well as protozoa smaller than itself. The food is digested inside its body in a special space called a vacuole.

Several species of worms live in the water or mud of ponds. Some are parasites living in the bodies of fishes and frogs, and others in birds, insects, crustaceans and molluscs. The best known is the leech, with its bare, ringed elastic body. It has two suckers with which it can attach itself to the host animal.

The medicinal leech pierces the skin of a fish with its suckers, which are lined with about a hundred pointed teeth, and sucks the fish's blood for food. The adult leech takes blood

great crested newt

tadpoles

water spider

great pond snail

caddis worm

water scorpion

swan mussel

from mammals. It can take in as much as 10 cm³ (½ fl oz) and can live on that for more than a year.

There are also several molluscs living in pools and ponds. Limnaea, the pond snails, are dark brown. They crawl around on leaves and submerged stems, or on the bottom. They nibble at aquatic plants and some also feed on the dead bodies of animals. Planorbis, another pond snail, is also herbivorous. It has a coiled but fairly flat shell. The biggest freshwater molluscs belong to the group called bivalves. Their shell, like that of mussels and oysters, consists of two parts, each part being called a valve. These are joined by a hinge. The shell can be opened or shut by the action of powerful muscles in the bivalve's body.

The swan mussel lives on the muddy bottoms of ponds and rivers. The inside of its shell is pearly and the outside is marked with concentric lines, each line representing a period of growth. This creature can live for several tens of years. The female lays anything up to 300,000 eggs per year. She keeps them between her valves. The larvae which hatch from the eggs attach themselves to the bodies of fishes for between two and ten weeks before they begin to lead an independent life. The swan mussel

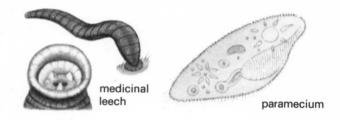

medicinal leech

paramecium

moves about in the mud, leaving tracks like furrows behind it. One of its enemies is the musk rat, which chews its shell off and eats the flesh inside.

The female mosquito lays her eggs in little rafts of about 300,000 eggs on the surface of the water. The raft breaks up when the eggs hatch. The larvae and pupae of mosquitoes live in the water. The adult female bites a mammal or a bird and sucks its blood. She cannot lay her eggs until she has had this feed of blood.

Long-legged insects called pond skates can often be seen skimming along on the surface of ponds, rivers and pools. Using only their second and third pairs of legs, they move over the water without sinking. Where the insect's feet touch, they make very slight hollows in the surface. The weight of the insect is so slight that the surface of the water is not broken.

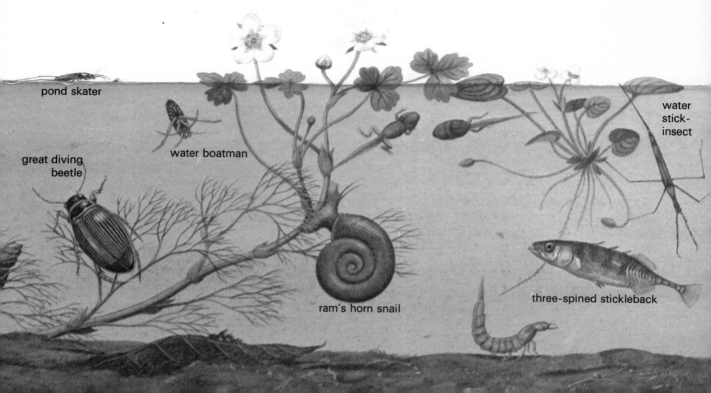

pond skater

water stick-insect

great diving beetle

water boatman

ram's horn snail

three-spined stickleback

pike

Still Waters:
Fishes and Frogs

Out of 20,000 species of fishes living throughout the world, just over 8,000 live in the fresh water of rivers and lakes. Just as the fox preys on fieldmice and the sparrowhawk on small birds, so the pike plays the role of predator in lakes and rivers. It is a carnivorous fish, eating ducklings as well as other kinds of fishes, especially young ones. It is cannibalistic, too, eating other smaller fishes of its own kind. The female pike is bigger than the male and can grow as big as 1.5 m (5 ft) long and 24 kg (52 lb) in weight.

Most fishes have scales. A pike, for example, has about 10,000. By looking at one of these through a magnifying glass, it is possible to estimate the animal's age from some quite wide lines which correspond to the summer period of growth, and other narrower, more crowded lines corresponding to the winter period. These lines are like the growth rings in the trunk of a tree.

A study of growth rings tells us that the carp can live to a maximum of forty-four years and can reach a weight of 30 or 40 kg (65–90 lb). But as the carp is favourite game for fishermen,

it is very rare that such an old one is found. The carp likes calm, warm water with an average temperature of between 21 and 25°C (70–77°F). It eats all kinds of things: little animals (insect larvae, worms, crustaceans), the seeds and fruit of aquatic plants and so on. Its diet varies according to the seasons. In the breeding season a female carp and one or several males swim together. As she lays her eggs, the female twists her body and stirs up the shallow water. The number of eggs laid depends on the size of the fish, but it can be more than a million. About 50 per cent die for different reasons. In winter the carp hibernates at the bottom of its pool. It loses weight because it does not eat. By contrast, other fishes, such as the perch and trout, remain active in winter. The three-spined stickleback is one of the smallest freshwater fish. It is found in Europe, Asia and North America and is well-known for the fact that the male builds a nest in which the female lays her eggs. The male fish is in charge of making the nest and keeps watch over the eggs until they hatch.

The eel looks rather like a snake, but it has dorsal and anal fins which are very long, as well as two small pectoral fins. It lives in lakes, canals and rivers, but it breeds in the middle of the Atlantic Ocean, in a place known as the

Sargasso Sea, named after the seaweed which floats on the surface. The young eels travel back to the rivers from which their parents originally came. Those that go to the American rivers take a year on the journey. Those going to Europe take nearly three years. They may stay there for about ten years before returning to the sea to reproduce.

The musk rat is an example of the danger of taking animals from one part of the world to another. Originally from North America, the musk rat was introduced into Europe in the early years of the twentieth century. It builds a hut-like dwelling of sticks, the opening to which is under water. This big rodent feeds almost exclusively on aquatic plants and is particularly active at night. By its burrowing it damages the banks of rivers and lakes.

The male edible frog is especially noisy on summer evenings when it croaks. With each croak, two little transparent sacks in the corners of its mouth swell up, making the sound carry a long way. These frogs are called amphibians because they lead a double life. As young frogs, they live in the water, but when they are fully grown they spend half of their time on land.

The edible frog breeds for the first time when it is three or four years old. This is the frog that is caught and eaten, especially in France. In May the female lays nearly 8,000 eggs from which hatch legless larvae, called tadpoles. They swim by waving their flat tail. On the

carp

musk rat

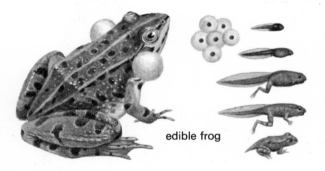

edible frog

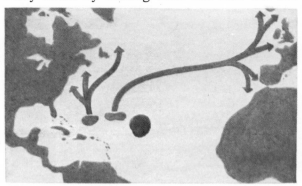

Above: A map of the North Atlantic Ocean showing where eels breed. The red arrows show the journey taken by the young of the European eel, the blue arrows show the journey taken by the young of the American eel.

three-spined stickleback (male, female and nest)

sides of their head they have feathery gills with which they absorb the oxygen dissolved in the water. These tadpoles undergo a gradual change. After three or four months their hind-legs appear, then their front legs, and then the tail gradually shrinks and they begin to look like little frogs. Their gills also disappear and are replaced by lungs. Finally, the intestine shortens. These changes in bodily structure are part of the process called metamorphosis.

85

Still Waters: Birds

In Europe in spring, non-migratory birds like the moorhen, or waterhen, the little grebe and the water-rail settle down to nest on or near to ponds. They are joined by migratory birds such as the great reed-warbler and the garganey, a kind of duck, which have returned from tropical Africa. Some choose the reeds, while others, like the coot and the crested grebe, make their nest on the edge of open water.

Between March and June the wild duck or mallard lays from seven to twelve eggs and sits on them for twenty-eight days. When they hatch, the ducklings are covered in down. Their eyes are open and they go swimming with their mother almost immediately. The male takes little part in looking after the ducklings. Mallard eat anything they can find – seeds, fruit, insects, molluscs, leaves and shoots of water plants.

The coot, often found on large lakes, is black with a whitish beak, a white shield on the front of its head and green legs. The moorhen, or waterhen, is smaller. It is blackish-brown with a white line on each side and has a red and yellow beak with a red shield on its face.

The great crested grebe needs wide open spaces of water and generally settles on large ponds. Its feet are webbed, but each toe is separate. This bird can dive to 5 or 6 m (16–20 ft) and travel as much as 20 m (65 ft) under water before coming up again. The great crested grebe builds a floating nest and the female sometimes carries her babies around on her back when they are a few days old. In February and March, which is mating time, male and female meet with noisy cries and go through a mating ritual. Sitting facing each other, they shake their heads, dive and bring to the surface pieces of water plants which they present to each other, standing straight up in the water breast to breast. In all this, the birds move in perfect time with each other.

The reed bunting and the great reed warbler are perching birds. The nest of the great reed warbler is slung between three or four stems.

mallard duck with ducklings

teal

mallard drake

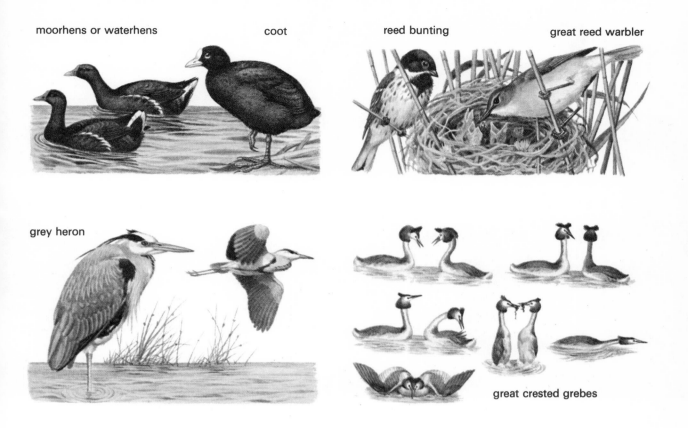

moorhens or waterhens

coot

reed bunting

great reed warbler

grey heron

great crested grebes

Left: Male and female great crested grebe in their spectacular courtship display rise out of the water breast to breast, each holding a piece of food in its beak.

saddlebill stork

white pelicans

Nile crocodile

Tropical Freshwaters

The freshwater rivers of the Tropics are ideal for large aquatic reptiles. Because they are always warm, crocodiles, caimans and alligators live in the swamps and rivers of Africa, Asia, America and Australia. Crocodiles differ from alligators in that they have a longer snout, and the fourth tooth in the lower jaw can still be seen when the mouth is shut. The Nile crocodile likes gently sloping river banks where it can sun itself and where the female can find a place for her nest. Each male fights to defend his own small territory which runs across the water from one bank to the other. Mating takes place in the water. Up to ninety eggs are laid in a pit about 60 cm (2 ft) deep, which the female hollows out with her front feet. She then covers the hole with sand and rotting plants. Incubation, guaranteed by the heat of the sun, lasts around twelve weeks. During this time the female stays near the nest and defends it fiercely against a large lizard called the Nile monitor which eats crocodile eggs. When they are ready to hatch, the young crocodiles call from inside the shell and mother helps them out. They are 20 to 30 cm (8–12 in) long and weigh 50 to 80 g (2–3 oz).

The hippopotamus is the largest freshwater mammal. It lives only in Africa. It leads a double life, for it is amphibious. During the day it stands in the water to shelter from the sun, with only its eyes, nostrils and ears showing. From time to time it dives and walks about on the bottom and then comes up to the surface after about four minutes. At night it goes ashore and grazes on tall grass in nearby fields. It can eat 70 kg (150 lb) of food in one night. The baby hippo is usually born on the river bank at the water's edge, but soon goes into the water. The hippo has huge lower canine teeth 50 to 60 cm (20–24 in) long, which are used for fighting. A hippo may live for forty-five years.

scissorbill

hammerhead

sandpiper

hippopotamus

Fighting between male hippos is an awesome sight as they rise out of the water with their huge mouths open, each trying to bite the other.

The big lakes and swamps of tropical Africa are a real paradise for birds and are the home of many species all year round. During October and November, millions of waders fly in from Eurasia and spend several months there.

The flamingo lives in large colonies scattered over tropical and subtropical regions of Europe, Asia, Africa and also southern Europe. Flamingoes live exclusively in saltwater or brackish lakes, and lagoons, and they make a nest measuring 15 to 46 cm (6–18 in), on which the female lays usually a single egg. In East Africa the lakes of the Rift Valley are inhabited by 3 to 3½ million flamingoes. They eat insect larvae, small crustaceans, molluscs and algae that live in the water or in the mud. They hold their beaks upside-down in shallow water and filter out their food.

The saddle bill of Africa is a large stork living on the edges of freshwater rivers and lakes.

On the gravel banks and shady margins of rivers and lakes and along the coasts of America,

Africa and Asia, lives the skimmer or scissor-bill. It nests in colonies, sometimes of thousands of pairs, with the nests scattered over a wide area. Each nest is no more than a hollow in the sand about 20 cm (8 in) across where the female lays two to four eggs. The scissor-bill's upper beak is 12 to 35 cm (½–1½ in) shorter than the lower. This enables it to scoop up prey as it skims the surface of the water in flight.

flamingo

Mountains of Europe: Vegetation

The vegetation on the slopes of a mountain changes as we climb from the valley to the summit. At the foot of the mountain are meadows and fields, woods of deciduous trees such as the oak, hornbeam, chestnut and so on. Higher up are forests of conifers such as pine, fir, spruce and larch. Then come the alpine meadows with stunted trees, like arolla pines, and rhododendron bushes, and finally, from about 3,000 m (10,000 ft) up, the snow cap. The altitude of these different zones varies according to the slope of the sides of the mountains. Also on the warmer southern slopes the trees extend higher up the mountain.

larch

On certain mountains the boundaries between the zones are not clearly marked; for example the conifers may mingle gradually with the deciduous trees. Generally the plants become progressively smaller from the base to the summit. This is due to the temperature which is very low at high altitudes; to the force of the wind (which breaks and knocks over the tall plants); to the intensity of the sunlight; to the thickness of the snow in winter; and, finally to the thinness of the earth layer which is replaced by bare rocks and scree, making it very difficult for plants to find a root hold.

The only tree to grow tall at high altitudes is the larch. It can be identified by its sparse, light-green foliage, by its small cones and by the fact that in the autumn it changes colour — the needles turn yellow and drop off, unlike those of the fir and the spruce which stay on the tree for up to nine years and are renewed gradually. These trees remain permanently green, which is why they are called evergreens.

Most herbaceous plants of the mountain meadows flower in June and July. The big round yellow flowers of the kingcup open out beside streams and on the wet slopes of the

rhododendron

mountains. This plant is a member of the buttercup family.

Gentians are often thought to be typical mountain plants. Indeed, most of the blue-flowered species live only in the mountains, but others such as the yellow variety are found on the plains and plateaus, which are only 300

great yellow gentian

spring gentian

alpine snowbell

edelweiss

lady's slipper orchid

globe flower

saxifrage

or 400 m (1,000–1,300 ft) above sea-level. The yellow gentian has bunched flowers and very big leaves with clearly marked veins.

Edelweiss is less widespread and grows higher up, between 2,000 and 3,000 m (6,500–10,000 ft), in places which are often difficult to reach, being cut off by rocks. Because it is such an unusual and rare plant, it is unfortunately being picked by thoughtless visitors and is fast disappearing. Its tiny flowers are surrounded by leaves which have a whitish, cottony down also found on the other parts of the plant.

Lady's slipper is a magnificent orchid which flowers between May and July. Like other members of its family, it should never be picked because it is becoming more and more rare, even if it seems to be flourishing in some areas. Its name comes from the big yellow petal which looks like a slipper.

Several varieties of saxifrage grow in the cracks of rocks, on scree and in moraines, which are the stones pushed back by the glaciers. They can be found at the base of the mountain or up as far as 3,000 or even 4,000 m (10,000–13,000 ft). These little plants grow in thick clumps – cushions of tightly packed leaves which in the summer send out stalks with white or pink flowerets on them.

Soldanella is a little round-leafed plant with lilac flowers which bloom in alpine meadows from May onwards. Their petals have a fringed edge. They live between the 1,000 m and 3,000 m (3,000–10,000 ft) levels.

Last but not least is the rhododendron, which is a little evergreen shrub of the same family as heather and grows between the forest zone and the alpine meadows. It has glossy green leaves and pink or white flowers.

Mountains of Europe: Cold-Blooded Animals

Just as flora becomes more and more sparse the further you go up a mountain, so does the fauna become scarcer towards the snow-covered peaks. The only inhabitants of the snowy summits are a few species of primitive insects,

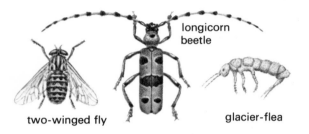

longicorn beetle

two-winged fly

glacier-flea

the best-known of which is the glacier-flea. This blackish little animal lives at an altitude of nearly 4,000 m (13,000 ft) and cannot bear temperatures higher than 10° or 12°C (50°–54°F). While other insects would die or hibernate at a temperature of −5°C (23°F), the

glacier-flea can continue to move about. It remains active all through the winter, under the snow where the temperature is about −2°C (29°F), and lives on pollen grains carried by the wind.

Much lower down, in clearings and on the borders of forests, can be seen a magnificent butterfly called the Apollo, the rear wings of which are tri-coloured. This is now a protected species in central Europe, because it was once a victim of fanatical collectors. The female lays her eggs in a white-flowered houseleek, a rare plant found above 1,500 m (5,000 ft). The chrysalis lives under a stone and the butterfly appears between June and September. It very rarely goes higher than 2,000 m (6,500 ft).

The erebus, with its black and white eye-spots, is another butterfly which has adapted to the mountains and high plateaus.

In the forest zone live insects which spend most of their lives under bark or in the trunks of beech trees and conifers. These are the wood-boring beetles. Their larvae feed on wood, which is indigestible and has very little food value. This explains why the larvae grow so slowly. Their intestine is full of single-celled animals or protozoa which break down the

alpine newt

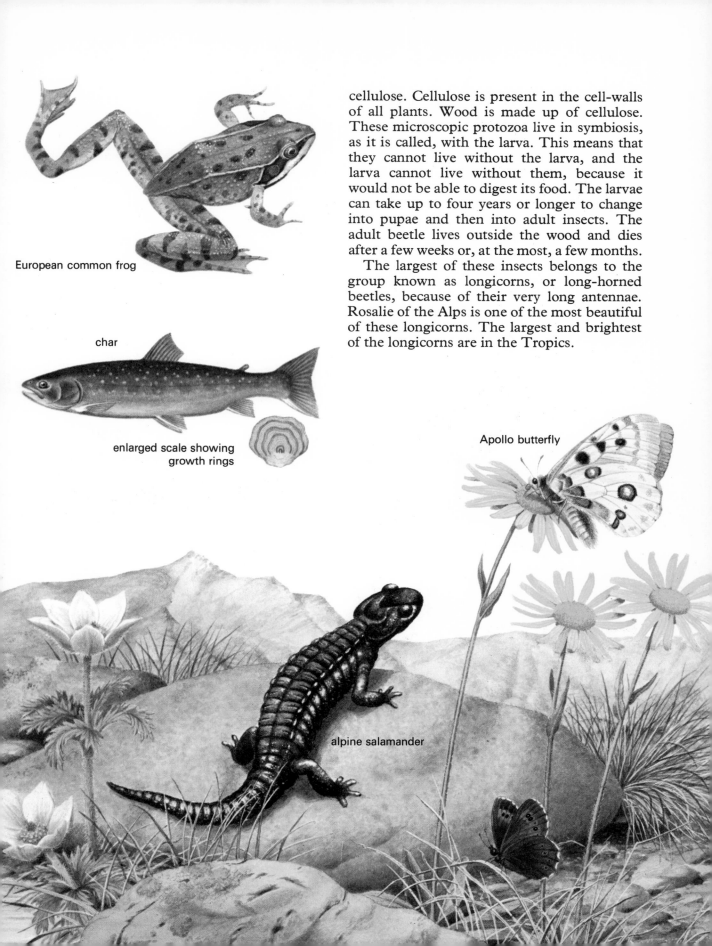

European common frog

char

enlarged scale showing
growth rings

cellulose. Cellulose is present in the cell-walls of all plants. Wood is made up of cellulose. These microscopic protozoa live in symbiosis, as it is called, with the larva. This means that they cannot live without the larva, and the larva cannot live without them, because it would not be able to digest its food. The larvae can take up to four years or longer to change into pupae and then into adult insects. The adult beetle lives outside the wood and dies after a few weeks or, at the most, a few months.

The largest of these insects belongs to the group known as longicorns, or long-horned beetles, because of their very long antennae. Rosalie of the Alps is one of the most beautiful of these longicorns. The largest and brightest of the longicorns are in the Tropics.

Apollo butterfly

alpine salamander

Mountains of Europe: Birds

The number of birds living exclusively in the mountains is very small. Among them, in Europe, are the ptarmigan, the snowfinch, the golden eagle, the nutcracker, the three-toed woodpecker and the black grouse.

In the spring months, May and June, the ptarmigan changes colour. Its plumage turns to a mottled black, white, beige and brown. The wings are the only parts which stay almost predominantly white. In October the bird moults again and regains its plumage, immaculate except for the black tail and the male's black eye-patch.

with its claws, or talons, knocking it out or tearing it into pieces with its beak. An eagle weighing 5 kg (11 lb) has great difficulty flying with prey that weighs any more than 1.5 kg (3 lb), so it chooses its victims carefully. To find food all year round, the eagle has to hunt over a huge area. This means that animals it feeds on in one part are left alone for a time so that they can breed and increase in number. The territory of a pair of eagles may be as large as 70 sq km (27 sq miles).

A golden eagle eats between 200 and 300 g (7–10 oz) of food at any one time, but it probably does not hunt every day. The female is larger and heavier than the male, but they both have the same colouring. They build their nest, or eyrie, amongst rocks in the shelter of an overhang. For several weeks at the end of

snowfinch

nutcracker

black grouse

ptarmigan

rock thrush

The golden eagle, so called because of the yellowish feathers on its head and nape, takes its prey by surprise as it flies not too far above the mountain slopes. It catches marmots mostly, but also mountain hares, young foxes, black grouse and ptarmigan. It seizes its prey

winter the two birds are busy piling up twigs, tufts of grass and small tree branches. The same nest is used off and on for a very long time, tens of years perhaps, and it grows and grows until it measures about 2 m (6½ ft) high and 1.5 m (5 ft) in diameter. The female lays

alpine swifts

The golden eagle and its eyrie on a ledge high in the mountains.

two eggs and sits on them for about forty-three days. The eaglets do not both hatch on the same day because the incubation period begins as soon as the first egg is laid, and the second egg comes two to five days later. The older chick is the stronger and it will sometimes stop the younger one from getting any food. The younger chick may then die of hunger. In this way the eagle population is maintained at a constant level and the surviving birds always have enough to eat.

Mountains of Europe: Mammals

Above the forests are the vast alpine meadows intersected by barriers of rock. This is the home of the chamois. A relative of wild goats, its coat changes colour with the seasons, from light brown in summer to black in winter. The coat also becomes thicker as it changes to black. The only parts which remain white all year round are the forehead and cheeks. Its two horns are hollow like those of sheep, domestic goats, cattle and ibex, and unlike the antlers of deer.

The chamois lives in herds made up of young ones not yet old enough to breed and females with their kids. The adult males live on their own except when mating time comes around in November and December. It is then that they drive away their rivals. The kids are born in May. The chamois eats nothing but plants. In the winter it goes down into the forests, where it is easier to find food, such as lichens, pine needles and ivy.

The golden eagle is the only natural enemy of the chamois. It attacks the kids, but these are defended by their mothers. It is mainly the newly born kids that are snatched, while they are still weak on their legs. The main dangers to chamois are hunger, winter avalanches, rock-falls and man.

The ibex is the biggest European mammal to live in the mountains, apart from the brown bear. It is found in the upper regions of the alpine meadows between 2,000 and 3,000 m (6,500–10,000 ft), where much of the surface is covered with rocks. Its long horns – as long as 90 cm (36 in) in males – have big grooves in them.

There are three small mammals which do not leave the mountain in winter. Despite the

marmot

snow vole

mountain hare

The marmot is one of the biggest rodents in Europe. It lives in colonies in burrows. Marmots can be seen in the meadows, in summer, at altitudes between 1,500 and 3,000 m (5,000–10,000 ft). Standing on its hindlegs, the marmot surveys its surroundings and if it sees a strange shadow it whistles, so warning other members of the colony, and then disappears quickly underground. In summer it cuts some grass, using its teeth, and leaves it to dry. Later, it carries this into its burrow. In the autumn it goes into hibernation – its body temperature drops, its heart beats very slowly and its breathing becomes so slow that it appears almost to be dead. This deep sleep lasts from October to March.

The mountain hare has shorter ears than the brown hare living on the plains. In summer it is brown, but in the autumn it becomes completely white except for the tips of its ears which stay black.

heavy snow and the cold, they manage to survive, each having its own way of escaping the rigours of winter. The marmot lives in the Alps and goes into hibernation deep in its burrow. The snow vole scurries about under the snow. The mountain hare grows a much thicker fur coat, and changes colour to white in winter so it is camouflaged against the snow.

chamois

ibex

97

sequoia or redwood

puma or cougar

bighorn

Rocky Mountains goat

mountain beaver

vicuña

guanaco

Mountains of America

The Pacific Ocean side of the Rocky Mountains receives a lot of rain – more than 2 m (6½ ft) per annum – which explains the lush vegetation on the smaller peaks such as the Sierra Nevada range. It is on these western slopes that the most remarkable of forest trees, the giant sequoias, are found. These conifers, famed for their huge size and for their long life-span, have been heavily exploited because of their high timber yield. Steps have now been taken to protect the largest of them as natural monuments. About thirty forests of these distinctive red-bark trees still remain, each containing anywhere between a few hundred and several thousand sequoias.

These trees can grow to be 3,000 years old. In one old tree that had been felled 3,100 growth rings were counted. A fully grown tree will measure between 80 and 100 m (260–330 ft) in height and 10 m (33 ft) in diameter at the base of the trunk. The weight of these giants has been estimated at 1,000 tonnes. The two biggest sequoias on record are 112 m (367 ft) and 110 m (361 ft) high. Another, nicknamed 'General Sherman' (a general in the American Civil War) is 83 m (272 ft) high, has a trunk measuring 11 m (36 ft) across and 31 m

(102 ft) in girth. Sequoias have a very fibrous bark which in the older trees can be up to 60 cm (2 ft) thick. The cones, on the other hand, are only 3.5 to 7.5 cm long (1½–3 in).

The Andes mountains run from one end of South America to the other. On either side of the median or central line of the mountains, at an altitude of between 3,600 and 4,200 m (11,800–13,800 ft), there stretches a vast plateau called the Puna. It is 200 km (125 miles) wide and 1,000 km (620 miles) long and overlooked by the mountains. There are no trees to be found on this high ground, but there are two species of camel, the guanaco and the vicuña which live in herds on the mountain pastures. The domesticated forms of guanaco and vicuña are much more numerous than the wild animals and are called respectively the llama and alpaca. The wild animals still survive in small numbers. The guanaco is the most widely found, from Peru to the north of Patagonia, and from sea level up to an altitude of 4,500 m (14,800 ft) in Peru. It lives in the desert, too, in the Atacama for example, where it hardly ever rains. The alpaca and vicuña both have a long neck, big ears and very thick fur which protects them from the cold, and the heat in the summer.

Of all the birds of prey, the condor is the one with the biggest wing span. There are two species – the Californian condor and the Andean condor. The Californian condor is gradually disappearing and there are only forty or fifty left now. One of the reasons for its decline seems to be that there are fewer cattle carcasses for them to eat. Nowadays farm animals are better cared for than in the past and the number that die from diseases is much reduced. The Californian condor has a wing

Condors, a kind of vulture, living high up in the Andes. When not perched on rocky ledges they soar high in the sky looking for dead animals to eat.

span of 2.85 m (9½ ft) and weighs 12 kg (26 lb). The wing span of the Andes condor is about 3 m (10 ft) or, if it is an exceptionally large bird, 3.23 m (10½ ft). This bird lives all through the Andes mountains, and from Peru onwards is often seen on the coast where it feeds on the carcasses of sea-lions to eat and eats the eggs of sea-birds. It nests on a cliff and the female lays a single white egg which is incubated for between fifty-four and fifty-six days.

The mountain beaver or sewellel is a large rodent found in the North American Rockies. Despite its name, it is not related to the beaver and lives in a burrow.

Mountains of Asia

On the southern slopes of the Himalayas, the highest mountain chain in the world, the forests of deciduous trees and conifers extend up to 3,500 m (11,500 ft). To the north of the mountain chain, however, there is much drier country extending into the deserts of Mongolia. The Himalayas and the plateaus of Tibet form an impassable barrier for many animals and only the migrating birds can cross it. They do so twice every year to winter on the plains of India of Indo-China, and then return to Siberia in summer.

There are some mammals such as the yak, the takin and the snow leopard which live permanently in the mountains. The wild yak has become rare, but the domesticated yak is very common in central Asia. It is related to the buffalo, the gaur, the anoa and other Asian cattle, but differs from them in the very long fur on its shoulders and sides to protect it from the wind and the cold. In summer the wild yak ascends to between 4,000 and 6,000 m (13,000–19,500 ft) to the alpine meadows, and eats only grass and herbaceous plants. In winter it comes down lower. It digs through the snow with its front hoofs to find dry grasses, moss and lichens.

The takin, a goat-antelope, never goes any higher than the rhododendron and bamboo zone in the south-east of the Himalayas. It is a very shy animal. Most takins have a dark brown coat, but in China there is a variety with golden yellow hair.

The snow leopard is one of the most beautiful of the big cats and also one of the least well known. In winter its fur becomes very long and silky and lighter than in summer, but is still covered in a pattern of big spots and rosettes about 7 or 8 cm ($2\frac{3}{4}$–3 in) across. It is widespread throughout Tibet, in the Himalayas, the Altai mountains, the Hindu Kush and part of Mongolia, but is rare in some of these regions. The snow leopard lives in the alpine meadows between 1,200 and 5,000 m (4,000–16,000 ft) in summer and comes down to the valleys in the winter. Its chief prey is the ibex, and occasionally wild sheep, but it also hunts marmots, hares, roe deer, rock partridges and pheasants. Its favourite times for catching its prey are at dawn and at dusk. During the day it dens up, usually in a cave or in the crevice of a rock.

From Afghanistan to the south of Tibet, the brilliantly-coloured monal lives in forests of oak and rhododendron broken up here and there with clearings. This short-tailed pheasant is a non-migrant bird and lives between 2,400

monal

bar-headed goose

ibisbill

eared pheasant

with rocks. Living here are some small perching birds such as the alpine accentor, a redstart and some pipits. In Nepal, these birds go up to 4,500 m (14,800 ft) and even as far as 5,300 m (17,400 ft). The three species of eared pheasants are widespread in the east of the Himalayas, Tibet and western China. The white-eared pheasant frequents the conifer forests at a height of between 3,200 and 4,200 m (10,500–13,800 ft). It can withstand temperatures as low as −35°C (−31°F) and does not come down below 3,000 m (10,000 ft). Outside the nesting season it stays in flocks of twenty to thirty birds, sometimes more.

There are few small animals living in the streams and on the banks of streams, as the fast-running current carries away those that have no suckers or other gripping organs. There are not very many birds either.

The falciroster lives on the banks of pebbles which clutter up the beds of streams between 2,000 and 4,000 m (6,500–13,000 ft) in Pamir, the Himalayas, Tibet and Manchuria. It is quite rare as it needs very special conditions. In China only eight pairs were counted over 7 km (4½ miles) of a stream. It is camouflaged by its shape, the form of its beak and its colour. It flies quite slowly, and the beating of its wings is like that of a seagull. This strange wader eats insects and larvae which it catches in the water.

and 5,000 m (8,000–16,000 ft). Its food consists of roots and bulbs which it pulls up with its beak, also shoots and berries. Pheasants are natives of Asia, but several have been introduced into Europe and elsewhere. Some, such as the Argus pheasant, live in tropical forests but some, like the silver pheasant, the golden pheasant and the eared pheasant, are mountain-dwellers.

Above the forests stretch the prairies, strewn

The rare and beautiful snow leopard that lives in the snowy heights of the mountains of central Asia.

yak

takin

giant panda

101

Mountains of Africa

There are forty-eight species of eagle in the world. All have claws and a hooked beak which they use to capture and tear their prey. From the Drakensberg Mountains in South Africa northwards to Egypt there are many summits and rocky peaks far above the plains, which are the home of Verreaux's eagle – one of the most powerful birds of prey. It lives as high as 3,300 m (11,000 ft) in Kenya and 4,000 m

inselbergs (small rocky summits) live the rock hydraxes, which are small mammals up to 80 cm (30 in) long. Although they look like rodents they differ from them in several ways and have been classified in a completely separate group or order. They have no tail, they have flat nails on their toes and on their back they have a large gland surrounded by yellow, black or white hair. These animals eat grass, mosses, leaves and fruit. They form colonies and live in rock crevices. Gestation lasts for at least seven months – as long as the brown bear!

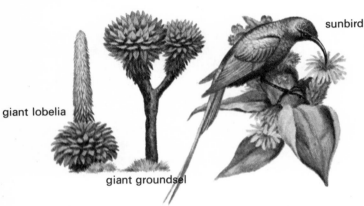

giant lobelia

sunbird

giant groundsel

Verreaux's eagle

(13,000 ft) in Ethiopia, seeking out rocky places. Each pair hunts over a territory of between 10 and 60 sq km (4–23 sq miles). The rock hyrax is its chief prey, but it also captures guinea fowl and dik-diks (small antelopes). The female lays one or two eggs but usually only one eaglet survives.

On the mountainsides in tropical Africa one can see almost the same belts of vegetation as in the Swiss Alps, but the plants grow much taller because of the warmer climate. Thus, the forests extend up to 3,000 m (10,000 ft) and at this altitude consist of bamboo, camphor-trees and juniper. Higher up are large areas of heathland and then the vegetation thins out. At about 4,500 m (14,800 ft) can be found the giant groundsels and lobelias. The lobelias, with their flowers grouped in tightly packed spear-like heads, look like tall candles. They attract small birds like the sun-bird or sugar-bird, which are perching birds resembling hummingbirds in their brilliant colours and in the way they feed on nectar and tiny insects.

On the rocky plateaus and up around the

No chamois are to be found in Africa, but the ibex lives in the Simien Mountains in Ethiopia and in the mountains on both sides of the Red Sea. Farther south, live the klip-springer and the mountain nyala. The klip-

bushbaby

hyrax

klipspringer

mountain nyala

A family of gorillas among the undergrowth on the slopes of a mountain in West Africa.

springer, an antelope, can take enormous leaps. It lives up to 3,900 m (12,800 ft) in Ethiopia and lower down on the peaks of central and south-east Africa. The mountain nyala, another antelope, of the mountains of southern Ethiopia, was discovered in 1908. It lives in the forests.

The mountain gorilla inhabits rain forests up to a height of 3,600 m (11,800 ft). There are only 300 left in the Virunga volcanoes area (Zaire-Rwanda) but the lowland gorillas still survive in large numbers. The gorilla's food consists of leaves, shoots, bark, stems, roots and fruit.

The mountain gorilla is a sociable animal and lives in groups of between seven and twenty-five under the leadership of an adult male. The rest of the group is made up of females and young gorillas. They walk on all fours and spend most of their time on the ground but the young gorillas climb about agilely in the trees. When in danger, they usually run away rather than fight. They spend a third of their time standing up in order to feed or to groom themselves. With the coming of evening, the gorillas prepare a nest for themselves, which they will use for a single night only. This nest is situated either on the ground or in the trees.

After they reach the age of six years the females have one baby every three or four years. They carry their baby in their arms until it is ten months old and look after it for one year.

Each group of gorillas moves about over an area of about 13 sq km (5 sq miles), but does not defend it; it is therefore not a true territory. The gorillas cover a considerable distance every day, stopping frequently to eat and rest.

The bushbaby or galago is a strange mammal related to the Madagascan lemurs. One kind of bushbaby lives in mountain forests up to a height of 3,500 m (11,500 ft) where it leads a nocturnal life. Its big, owl-like eyes are adapted to seeing in the dark. During the day it sleeps in the trees rolled up in a ball. It has a cry like that of a baby. It is a tree-dweller, but it comes down to the ground from time to time.

tree yucca

Deserts

Deserts occupy about one fifth of the world's land surface. The biggest are found in Africa (Sahara, Kalahari and Namib), in central Asia (Kazakstan, Mongolia), in Arabia, in North America, South America and in Australia.

Deserts are defined as those regions where the annual rainfall is less than 25 cm (10 in). Temperatures are generally high during the day – up to 56°C (132°F) in summer in the Sahara, the average being between 40° and 45°C (104°–113°F) – but at night it is often

A desert scene in south-western United States.

very cold. In the Sahara in winter it can get down to −10°C (14°F).

Because there can be months or even years between one rainfall and the next, the vegetation is sparse, if not absent altogether. The sand dunes occupy only a small area of the desert which consists mostly of wide open stretches covered in pebbles or rocks. The vegetation does not always tell us where the deserts begin or where the steppes or dry grasslands end, because the transition is gradual.

There are plants and animals living in the desert, but there are not very many different species. In the Sahara about 1,200 plant species have been counted, and in Arizona there are 68 species of cactus. All desert plants have adapted to cope with the extremes of temperature in their environment: the leaves have a smaller surface area or are reduced to spines. This limits the loss of water and prevents the plants from drying out. They also have very long roots which go deep into the sand to reach the water tables underground. The leaves of some desert plants (cactus and caper-bush) are protected by a waxy layer. Tightly packed hairs perform a similar function. Other plants, such as the cacti of the Mexican desert, store water in their stems which become succulent. The saguaro or giant cactus reaches a height of 15 m (50 ft), but its growth is very slow and only a few of these plants reach such a size.

In Africa spurges or euphorbias take the place of cacti. The two are similar in some respects. Palm trees, typical desert plants, are

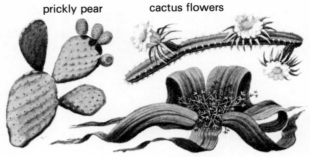

prickly pear   cactus flowers

Welwitschia

found not only in Africa, but also in America, although they are not numerous – in the Colorado desert there are only about 11,000. The prickly pear or Barbary fig is more common.

The flowers of the yucca are grouped at the top of a tall stem which is surrounded by long, stiff, pointed leaves. The plant is pollinated by a special nocturnal moth.

sand skink   scorpion

saguaro

Deserts of Africa and Asia

There are some large mammals which manage to survive in the desert. The best-known is the one-humped or Arabian camel which no longer lives in the wild. The two-humped, or Bactrian camel lives in the deserts of central Asia, but has become very rare in the wild. In 1962 there were 80 counted in Mongolia and the total number remaining would be between 400 and 500.

The Arabian camel is a domesticated animal and now lives only in this state. It is able to withstand heat and lack of water. It can lose up to 40 per cent of the water contained in its tissues, while other animals die if they lose 20 per cent. It makes up for the temporary dehydration when it reaches an oasis. Then it takes in huge quantities of water, and can drink 90 l (20 imp gal, 24 US gal) at a time! The water is stored neither in its hump, which is a fat reserve, nor in the stomach. It is distributed throughout the entire body. The camel is also able to economize on the amount of fluid it loses. Its temperature can rise from 34°C at night to 41°C (93°–106°F) during the day, and yet it will sweat very little. Its coat also protects it from loss of heat. The hairs may be 70° or 80°C (125–145°F) in the direct sun, but the temperature at the base of the hairs will only be 40°C (102°F).

In the deserts and arid steppes of the Kazakhstan (western Siberia) lives the saiga antelope. Herds of these animals move about regularly, travelling vast distances to reach regions where the grass and mugwort are green. These movements could be called migrations – the comings and goings between two areas. The adult can run at speeds of 70 km (44 miles) per hour. The wolf, the antelope's main predator, cannot exceed 40 to 45 km (25–28 miles) per hour, but in winter it attacks the weak animals in the herd. In fact the chief cause of death among the antelopes is the bad weather with its snow and ice, and some years thousands of them die from lack of strength.

sandgrouse

lanner falcon

gerbil

horned viper

rosy-coloured starling

fennec fox

addax

saiga antelope

Mongolian gazelle

The addax is the only antelope capable of living permanently in the driest regions. It can go without drinking water and finds enough moisture in the plants it eats. Most of the small animals in the desert (fennec fox, jerboas, scorpions, insects, lizards and snakes) are active during the night. Thus, they are able to escape the burning rays of the sun and economize on water. They spend the daylight hours sheltering under a rock or in a burrow underground.

About the size of a mouse, jerboas can jump between 2 and 3 m (6–10 ft) in a single bound. This is because their hindlegs are longer and stronger than their front legs. They live in the north of Africa and in central Asia.

The fennec is a cousin of the fox and lives in the Sahara and in Arabia. With its big ears, which are about 15 cm (6 in) long, it can hear the slightest noises. These are often clues to the whereabouts of its prey.

The rose starling or rosy pastor is related to the common starling. They are alike in the way that they fly and in their sociable habits. The rose starling nests in the south-east of Europe, in Asia Minor and in central Asia. Its favourite food is crickets and it can eat 200 in one day.

The lanner falcon lives in the arid areas of Africa, Arabia and the Balkans. It hunts pigeons, larks and occasionally lizards and rodents.

A group of the Asiatic or Bactrian camels shown in a natural setting in the deserts of central Asia.

Deserts of America and Australia

The deserts of North America (Sonora, Mohave, Grand Canyon), of Mexico and of South America, between the Andes mountains and the Pacific Ocean, are thought of as warm deserts. In North America the best known of the snakes living in the arid areas of Arizona, California, Nevada and Colorado is the rattlesnake. This snake hunts birds and rodents. At the end of its tail it has a horny rattle and every time it sheds its skin one more piece is added to the rattle. When the snake is disturbed, it lifts its tail and vibrates the rattle. Like all snakes it renews its skin two or three times a year. Usually in a snake the old skin peels off all in one piece, and the snake gets rid of it by rubbing its body along the ground. In a rattlesnake the end piece is left behind and makes one more ring to the rattle.

The burrowing owl frequents the prairies and dry places from the south of Canada to the Arctic regions. In California it can be found

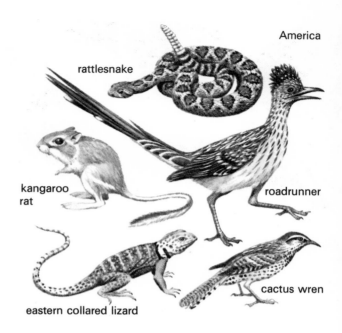

wherever there are burrowing mammals, especially a rodent called the gopher which digs holes for itself. Once a hole has been abandoned by its owner, the owl moves in, but it will never take over one that is already inhabited. This owl is rather like the little owl

The galah or roseate cockatoo is a native of Australia. The bird was once found only in dry inland areas, but has now spread to many parts of Australia.

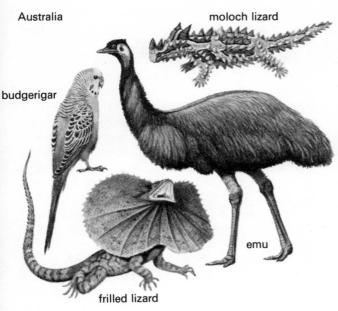

Australia

budgerigar

moloch lizard

frilled lizard

emu

of Europe, but it has longer feet. It eats insects, scorpions and lizards.

Another rather strange-looking bird, which is in fact a non-parasitic cuckoo, is the road-runner. It was given this name because it moves by walking or running rather than flying, most

of the time. Taking big steps, it can reach a speed of 25 km (15 miles) per hour. With its beak it catches insects, lizards and small snakes. Its nest, which it builds in a bush, contains between three and six eggs.

There are no large mammals in the deserts of North America. They are all small or medium-sized, with predators such as the puma and the lynx, or rodents like the prairie-dog and the kangaroo rat.

Kangaroo rats can be compared with the jerboas of Africa and Asia. They live in burrows and only come out at night. Covering about 20 to 50 m (65–165 ft), they collect seeds in their cheek-pouches and then go back into their burrows. When they are moving about slowly they use all four feet, but when they want to go faster they jump on their hindlegs. They can jump a distance of 2 m (6 ft) and a height of 60 cm (2 ft).

In Australia there are neither true cats nor carnivores of the wolf family, except for the dingo. This is a wild dog which is thought to have been introduced to this continent by the first aboriginal settlers. The wild budgerigar lives in flocks nesting in a hole in a tree.

The burrowing owl is found in North America and Canada. It eats insects and lizards and sometimes small rattlesnakes.

Domestic Mammals

It is difficult to determine how long ago certain farm animals were domesticated. We know the facts about some of them, such as the rabbit, turkey and guineafowl, but as for the cow or the horse, the change from the wild state to a domestic existence happened a very long time ago and we cannot say exactly when. This change did not happen overnight. It must have taken centuries of patient effort to tame such animals and change the temperament and physical make-up of those species which were important to man. After a careful selection process, man has succeeded in breeding races of animals which, within a species, differ in size and shape, colour and their ability to perform certain tasks. These races always belong to the same species and it is always possible for members of two races to breed.

The horse was domesticated at least 3,000 years ago. There are very few existing now in the wild state – just a few living on the steppes of central Asia. The biggest horses, known as draught- or shire-horses, weigh more than a tonne and reach a height of nearly 2 m (17 hands) at the withers. In contrast are the small Icelandic ponies which vary in height from 60 cm to 1 m (2–3 ft). In between the two is the saddle-horse which measures up to 1.65 m ($5\frac{1}{2}$ ft) and weighs 500 kg (1,100 lb). The maximum speed that a race horse can reach is about 64 km (40 miles) per hour for short distances. Male horses able to reproduce are called stallions; the females are called mares. The young horse is called a foal. It is born after a gestation of eleven months (gestation is the length of time that it takes for the baby to develop inside its mother).

Cattle are thought to have come from the aurochs, a wild ox with big horns which was still living in Europe at the beginning of the Middle Ages. The last of the wild species died in Poland in the seventeenth century. Bullocks are males which have been castrated when young – that is, they have been given an operation to make them unable to breed. Cow's milk is produced by her mammary glands to nourish the calf. The calf feeds from its mother by sucking at one of her teats. The mother has four teats, one on each mammary gland. The dairy shorthorn is one of the commonest breeds in Britain and it has been exported to almost every country in the world except in the tropics. It is red, white or red and white and is useful for its milk yield and for its beef.

bull

cow

ram

sheep

goat

pig or hog

horse

The Friesian from the Netherlands is black and white and smaller, but also a very good milk-producer. Certain breeds have adapted to living in the mountains or in elevated pasture lands.

Sheep probably come from the wild sheep of Asia. Only the male, called a ram, has horns. The female, or ewe, can have a lamb when she is two years old. Through breeding, man has very gradually brought about a change in the skin of the sheep to develop a thick layer of fine, curly wool beneath the big thick fibres of its top coat. These enlarged fibres are what is called the wool or the fleece.

The goat is probably descended from the wild goat of western Asia which lives now on the Greek islands and in the Middle East (Iran and Turkey). It has been domesticated for about 5,000 or 6,000 years. Goats are raised for their meat and their milk which is also used to make cheese.

newborn rabbit

rabbit

Pigs have been farmed for possibly 10,000 years. They belong to the same species as the wild boar. The males of the biggest breeds reach a weight of 500 to 600 kg (1,100–1,300 lb). The young, called piglets, are born in litters of between six and twelve, after about 114 days. The female, called a sow, has between twelve and sixteen teats. The pig has the reputation of being dirty, but it is no dirtier than any other animal. However, like the wild boar, the pig does like to wallow in the mud to refresh itself.

Domestic Insects and Birds

Of all domestic animals, the honeybee is the one that has been the most studied. This social insect lives, usually in a hive, in colonies of between 40,000 and 100,000 insects consisting of three different castes – a queen, males or drones (a few hundred) and up to 60,000 workers. The workers are females that are unable to lay eggs. In the wild state bees make their home in such places as a hole in a tree or in a chimney. With the wax produced from glands in their abdomen, the workers construct combs made up of a network of hexagonal cells. Some will be filled with honey, some with pollen and in others the queen will lay her eggs in the spring at the rate of about 1,500 per day. The queen lives for four or five years, while the workers die after four or five weeks in the summer. During the winter they slow down and live for six months. The worker's life is very carefully regulated. The egg hatches after three days. The larva is then fed by the adult bees with royal jelly, a secretion from the glands in their head. At six days the cell is closed by a cap of wax and the larva changes into a pupa. Two weeks later the young bee comes out of its cell. The cell is cleaned by the workers and the queen lays another egg in it. For about seventeen days the young bee is busy

Honeybees attending to the comb. Some of the cells contain grubs which will one day turn into worker bees.

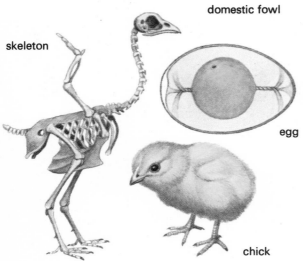

skeleton

domestic fowl

egg

chick

feeding the larvae and building new cells. It helps to clean the hive where a constant temperature of about 35°C (95°F) is maintained. When it is twenty days old, it leaves the hive to collect nectar and pollen. In one day it can cover 100 km (62 miles) in its comings and goings. Sometimes it will travel as far as 3 km ($1\frac{3}{4}$ miles) from the hive. When the honey-gatherers discover a new source of nectar, they return to the hive and dance to tell the other bees where the nectar is and encourage them to go in search of it. The dehydrated nectar will turn into honey which is used for food for the larvae and the adult bees.

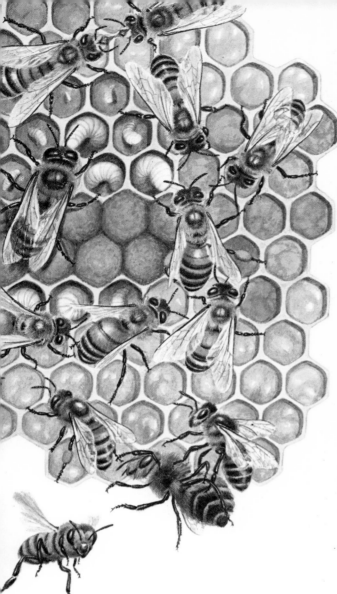

victim, it leaves its sting in the skin. In so doing, it is so badly wounded that it dies.

The domestic fowl is probably the most widespread species of bird because man has taken it to all parts of the world. The wild species from which it is descended is the red jungle fowl, which still survives in South-East Asia. It is similar to a bantam chicken. The domestic chicken is raised for its meat or for its eggs. The eggs we eat, with their white, brown or reddish shell, are not fertile, which means that they would not hatch into chicks.

Inside the egg there are two white membranes lying close together all the way round except at the big end where they separate to form an air space. Inside this membrane is a yellowish jelly-like substance called the albumen or 'white' and in the middle of this is the yolk on which rests the female cell or, if the egg has been fertilized, the embryo. The yolk provides food for the embryo which grows into a chick if the egg is incubated for twenty-one days and twenty-one nights at a temperature of 33° or 34°C (91°–93°F). The white acts as a cushion for the developing embryo. The incubation is carried out by the hen who sits on the eggs. To get out of the egg, the chick makes use of a white lump on the end of its beak, known as the egg-tooth. This falls off several days after the chick has hatched. The chicks are already covered with down when they hatch. They can see perfectly and can walk about as soon as their down is dry.

When the hive is heavily populated, some royal cells are constructed in which new queens are reared. The old queen leaves the hive with a party of workers, in search of a new place to live. This is known as swarming. In the hive the young queens that have hatched fight each other until only one is left alive. This queen mates with five or six males and in her turn starts to lay more eggs.

At the tip of its abdomen, a bee has a sting which it uses to defend itself. The sting is attached to a poison gland and is covered with tiny barbs which hold it in the skin when the bee stings. When the bee pulls away from its

turkey

domestic goose

guineafowl

domestic duck

goldfish

domestic cat

Household Animals

Living with us in our houses and flats are many little creatures which we generally find very annoying because they raid our food supplies, attack our clothes and settle in places which should be kept clean.

The housefly resists all attempts at destroying it. It reproduces at an extraordinary rate – there are eight generations of fly per year and the female lays between 600 and 1,000 eggs which she deposits in bags of 100 to 200 on our food, especially on meat. After two days the larvae (maggots) hatch out and, for about a week, they grow until they change into pupae in the ground. They remain in this state for up to three weeks. The insect which emerges lives for two to four weeks in the summer but longer in the winter. The fly feeds with its proboscis sucking in all kinds of liquid substances – milk, jam, syrup and sweat. As it passes from one substance to the next, it leaves behind microbes which are often dangerous to human health. This is why flies should be destroyed. The fly's wings beat at a rate of 200 beats per second. It can move about on vertical surfaces as slippery as glass, or upside-down on the ceiling. Its feet are covered in tiny hairs which act like suckers gripping any tiny rough spots on the surface.

Another unpleasant little insect is the clothes moth, which lives a more hidden life than the

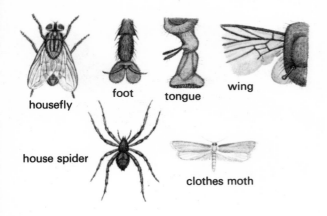

housefly   foot   tongue   wing

house spider   clothes moth

that are not opened very often, or under the eaves of houses, lives an enemy of the housefly. This is the house martin, a migratory bird which spends the winter in Africa, south of the Sahara and comes back to Europe in April. It builds its nest with little balls of mud which it picks up in its beak from the edges of puddles and streams. The male and female both share this work which goes on for about ten days. The final nest is cup-shaped with an opening at the top. The martins line the nest with dry grasses and lots of feathers. Then in May or June the female lays four or five white eggs which hatch after twelve to fifteen days. As soon as the young are hatched, the parents go to and fro (eight to fifty times an hour depending on the size and the number of babies) in search of food. The young martins fly from the nest when they are twenty days old. The adult catches

housefly. In summer especially, little flying insects can be seen in the house, but their metamorphosis cannot usually be seen. The clothes moth belongs to a family numbering about 2,000 species throughout the world. Some live on animal hair (such as sheep's wool)

house mouse

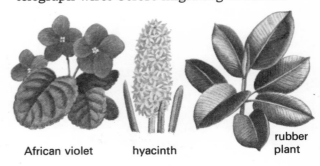

feral pigeon

house martin

others on animal horns, grain, lichen, moss or feathers. The female lays 60 to 100 eggs and these hatch into little grubs which chew at the substance on which they find themselves. The grubs turn into moths over a period of four to twelve months. The clothes moth's worst enemies are light and cold, and it also dislikes being disturbed.

The house spider, or Tegenaria atrica weaves its web in the angle of walls in dark rooms and cellars. Then it waits for an insect to pass by, which may be a long time. Spiders weave their webs of silk which is produced by glands in their abdomen. They kill their victims with a poisonous bite.

Under balconies, in the corners of windows

little insects which are blown along on the wind: flies, mosquitoes and midges. It accumulates dozens (as many as 380) of these creatures in its gullet before carrying them back to its young. In August the swallows gather together on the telegraph wires before migrating to Africa.

African violet   hyacinth   rubber plant

tortoiseshell
butterfly

peacock
butterfly

cabbage white
butterfly

house sparrow   starling

Animals in the Garden

In spring and summer the garden is visited by
several kinds of butterfly. In Europe there is the
white cabbage butterfly, the peacock butterfly,
which has large eye-spots on its wings, and the
tortoiseshell which sometimes takes refuge in
houses for the winter. The caterpillar of the
cabbage white butterfly devours the leaves of
the cabbage plant, while other caterpillars feed
on the leaves of nettles.

The greenfly and blackfly have a proboscis
called a rostrum, which they plunge into the
stems of plants to suck up the sap. There are
about 5,000 species of ladybird. The larvae and

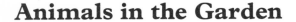

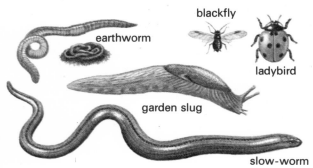

blackfly

earthworm

ladybird

garden slug

slow-worm

the adults eat the greenfly in large numbers.
Some ladybirds are red with two black spots,
some have seven dark spots and others are
yellow with black spots.

The leaves of lettuce and other vegetables
are eaten by slugs. The smallest, called grey
field slugs are a marbled black or grey and black,
and reach the same size as the big red slugs
which are found in the forest. Slugs are molluscs
like snails, but they are shell-less or their shell
is small and thin and covered with a loose flap
of skin called the mantle. Their eyes are at the
ends of two small tentacles which can be with-
drawn. Slugs move about on the ground or on
plants by wave-like movements in their muscular 'foot'. This is coated with a sticky slime
which leaves a shining trail when it dries. They
feed by scraping off small pieces of leaf with a
rasp-like tongue. They breathe by means of a
lung which opens to the outside by a small
round hole which is visible on the side of the
body.

The blackbird is very common in gardens,
but is more timid than the house sparrow. The
male is all-black with an orange bill, the female
and young are mainly brown. From January
onwards the male begins to sing, perched on a
tree or wall. He can be heard singing until July.
In March and April he is so busy helping to
feed the first nestful of babies that he may only
be heard at dawn. The blackbird's nest is well
hidden and made of a wall of moss and dry
grass reinforced inside with mud and dry grass.
There are four to six eggs bluish-green and
spotted with chestnut. They are incubated by
the female. The blackbird eats fruit, insects,
small snails and earthworms which it pulls out
of their holes.

There are many species of earthworms.

blackbird

Usually they are 10 to 25 cm (4–10 in) long, but the giant earthworms of Australia may be over 3 m (10 ft) long. Earthworms come regularly to the surface on wet nights to gather bits of dead leaves which they drag into their holes. The body of the earthworm consists of numerous segments or muscular rings which the animal expands and contracts in order to move about. Earthworms are very important for they aerate the ground by hollowing out tunnels. They also enrich it with decayed vegetable matter. The worm-casts which appear on the surface of the ground are the worm's waste material or excrement. The earthworm is hermaphrodite, which means that each one is both male and female but two worms must come together before either of them can lay eggs. From each egg, enclosed in a cocoon, hatches a young worm. Towards the front end of a worm's body is a slightly thickened part. This is called the saddle. It is often said this is where the worm has been cut in two by a spade and each half has re-grown the missing part. This is not true. The saddle gives out a fluid that hardens to form the cocoon for each egg as it is laid.

Garden Plants

The plants that we grow in our gardens have come from many parts of the world. The green bean came from South America, rhubarb from central Asia, the pumpkin from tropical America, the melon from tropical Asia and the cucumber from India. The pear and the quince are natives of the Middle East, the peach was imported from China, the apricot and the almond from Asia.

Garden vegetables have been selected by man for their tasty fruits, roots or leaves. Their seeds are carefully harvested for future crops, but some plants can be propagated in other ways as well. Normally, plants reproduce by means of the seeds from their flowers, but several, like the strawberry, send out creeping stems or runners which later grow roots, separate from the mother plant and form new and independent plants. One has only to cut a shoot from a geranium plant and put it in soil in a pot, to make a new plant; the roots grow quickly on the cut section of the stem. This technique is called 'taking cuttings'. Woody plants like the cherry tree and the grape vine are grafted; that is, a shoot is fixed into another plant and takes growing strength from it.

The roots which hold vegetables in the ground take a different form from one species to another. The root of the carrot, swollen with nutritive substances, is called a tap root because it is thick and goes deep into the earth. The carrot which we eat is the main root on which grow secondary rootlets. The runner bean, however, has fibrous roots, resembling a small bundle of twigs. A lettuce which is not picked and is left to grow sends out a tall stem at the

roses

lupins

iris

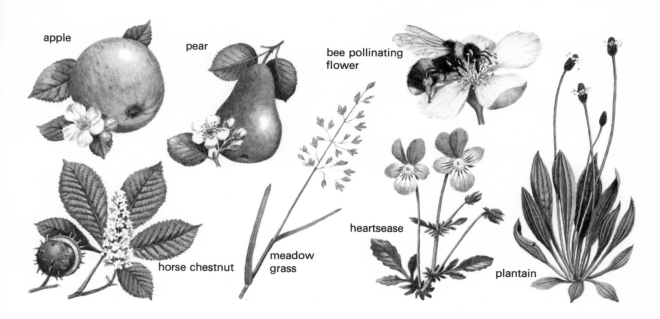

apple

pear

bee pollinating flower

horse chestnut

meadow grass

heartsease

plantain

top of which appear flowers. When a vegetable plant does this, it is said to have gone to seed. Some lettuces have frilly leaves and others have smooth ones. Cabbage lettuce is the frilled variety, while the cos lettuce has long, straight, smooth-edged leaves.

The flowers of the apple, plum and cherry trees are pollinated by honey-gathering insects, especially bees and bumblebees. The pistils of these plants cannot generally be fertilized by pollen from the same flower because it does not become mature at the same time as the ovules (female cells). For fertilization, and thus fruit production, to take place, the pollen must be transported from the stamens of one flower to the pistil of another flower by insects. Without them there would be practically no fruits. The apple is a fruit with pips; pips are seeds which are encased in a tough, brown skin. The cherry on the other hand is a stone fruit. Part of the stone is woody and hard. Inside the nut is the seed or kernel. Apples and cherries are fleshy fruits. The bean pod, however, is a dry fruit which contains several seeds. The seed of the bean has inside it a tiny root, a stalk and a growing point which is surrounded by nourishing substances for the new plant. It will germinate if it is placed in the earth in spring. When the young bean shoot appears on the surface, the seed rises with it but separates into two parts, the cotyledons, between which are two

small leaves called 'seed leaves'. Little by little, the cotyledons dry out and shrivel, emptied of their food reserves.

The horse chestnut is an ornamental tree, reaching a height of 25 m (80 ft). It grows rapidly in damp soil. Each of its leaves consists of leaflets arranged like the fingers on a hand on the end of a leaf-stalk, the whole being about 20 cm (8 in) across. The green fruits, covered in a husk bearing sharp spikes, have a big brown seed inside, with a whitish band at the top. This is called a chestnut. It is not edible, but it does have pharmaceutical uses. The horse chestnut has white flowers and blooms in April and May. It is a native of Asia Minor and Eastern Europe, and was introduced to Britain about 1650. The red-flowered chestnut is less widespread. It comes from North America.

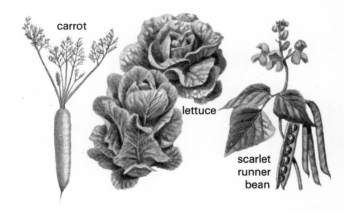

carrot

lettuce

scarlet runner bean

European Farmlands

By planting a single crop, such as wheat, over wide areas, man has created an unnatural environment which suits certain plants and animals but is harmful to others. All the work in the fields, including the ploughing, harrowing, spraying of chemicals to kill pests such as insects, worms and fungi, and the harvesting, has a devastating effect on the environment and the animals and plants that used to live there. Species unable to tolerate the changes disappear – at least for a time – being forced to live on the edges of their natural territory, and to adapt themselves accordingly.

However, if man were not to take so much care over his crops, they would degenerate and become like the wild species from which they are descended. What is more, the fields would be invaded by wild plants and these would take over from the cultivated plants. So we find that there are relatively few animals and wild plants in the cultivated fields, compared with

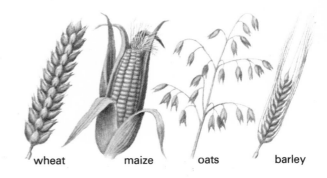

wheat   maize   oats   barley

the number found in meadows and woods. On the other hand, the soil is a haven for a great number of micro-organisms (plants and animals that can only be seen with a microscope). There may be hundreds of millions of bacteria, for example, in a single gram of earth!

Wheat is thought to have come from western Asia originally. Numerous varieties have been grown to obtain more grain of a bigger size and stalks which will not flatten in heavy rain. Some varieties of wheat are bearded, that is, they have a silky tuft at the end of the ear which makes them look similar to barley. Wheat is sown

tree sparrow

harvest mouse

either in autumn or spring and rich earth.

Barley, called winter barley if it is sown in autumn, can be distinguished from wheat by its narrower, more tightly packed grains, the long silk 'beards' on its heads and the fact that it does not usually grow as tall. Oats are easy to recognize because each grain hangs on the end of a little stalk. Maize is a South American plant which was introduced into Europe in 1520. For a long time it grew only in the south-west and the south-east where it had plenty of the necessary warmth and water. Now it is grown everywhere because hybrid varieties have been bred which can stand a colder climate. These varieties still need plenty of water though. The green spindles which can be seen on the stalks in July contain the female flowers. These give rise to the ears of corn from each of which hangs a bunch of reddish-brown fibres called stigmas. The male flowers are like yellow plumes.

There are several mammals and birds which are considered to be pests in the cultivated fields because they eat the grain or the green parts of the plants, or because they knock down

cornflower   larkspur

the seedlings and nibble at the roots. One of these is the mole. It spends all its life underground, digging tunnels with its broad front feet. It heaps the excavated earth up on the surface of the ground where it forms mole-hills which give away the mole's presence underground. The mole's eyes are so tiny that they perceive only the difference between light and darkness.

Over much of Europe the crested lark can be found in fields of beet and cereal crops, and in all dry places. It is larger than the skylark and can be recognized by the tuft on its head. It makes its nest in a hollow in the ground, and in May it lays between three and five spotted eggs which the female sits on for thirteen days. This lark does not migrate.

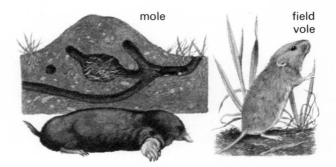

mole   field vole

In the autumn and during the winter, big flocks of rooks invade the fields. They are joined by many other rooks flying in for the winter from northern Europe. These birds return to their homeland at the beginning of spring. The rook eats grain, worms and insect larvae, especially wireworm and cockchafer grubs. It is a sociable bird and nests in colonies.

The bustard is a smaller edition of the great bustard which used to live in Britain until it was exterminated by being shot. The little bustard lives on the flat country of southern Europe.

The tree sparrow is related to the house sparrow from which it differs in having a chocolate-coloured crown instead of a grey crown. It lives in holes in trees on the edges of villages. In some parts of Europe the tree sparrow is more numerous than the house sparrow and it there becomes as great a pest in cornfields as the house sparrow is in Britain, eating large quantities of grain.

little bustard

crested lark   rook

Fields and Hedgerows

The potato came originally from the Andes mountains in South America. It was introduced into Europe in the sixteenth century, and was first thought of as a curiosity or a decorative plant with its white, pink or mauve flowers. But it came to play a very important role in the human diet. Its green fruits are poisonous, but its tubers, which are swollen underground stems, are edible and also sprout to form other potato plants. If potatoes are put in the ground in March or April, about 10 cm (4 in) below the surface, they will sprout up to twenty

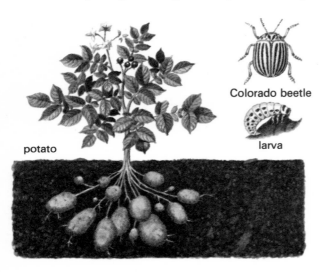

potato

Colorado beetle

larva

shoots. It is not necessary to sow seed in order to grow more potato plants. The tubers have a fine yellowish or pink skin, depending on the variety. They are harvested in September or October, unless they are 'new' potatoes which are dug at the beginning of summer or even earlier. Fields of potatoes are weeded to prevent the spread of harmful plants which could take over from them.

The colorado beetle lays its oval, yellowish eggs ten to eighty at a time on the undersurface of potato leaves. After a few days the reddish, black-spotted larvae hatch. At the end of three weeks they are 15 mm ($\frac{5}{8}$ in) long, and they eat the leaves down to the veins. The pupa lives in the ground for between eight and fifteen days

beet   sunflower   rape

before the adult emerges from it. This beetle can live for eighteen months to a year and hibernates twice. The adult insects of the last generation of the year bury themselves in the ground to hibernate. This beetle, which does great harm in potato fields, reached Europe from America in 1877. It has been stamped out in Britain.

Several varieties of beet are cultivated as food crops for humans and animals. Sugar beet is made into sugar cubes or crystallized sugar, while red beetroot is a vegetable grown especially for the table. Swedes or mangold-wurzels are given to cattle in the winter. They are stored in clamps, long pits covered with straw and other materials which protect them from frost. A wild variety of the plant grows on the shores of the Atlantic and the Mediterranean. It has tiny greenish flowers which are hardly noticeable.

Several years ago the cultivation of sunflowers became widespread in parts of Europe. Before this time, the sunflower, which came from North America, was grown in gardens as

thistle

furze or gorse

large stinging nettle

a purely decorative plant. It has very big flowers, about 30 cm (12 in) across. The receptacle, or swollen part of the flower, is filled with black seeds which contain a nourishing oil.

In May the fields of rape burst into flower and cover the countryside with a beautiful carpet of bright yellow. Rape is sown at the end of summer or in the spring, and is harvested in July. Its seeds are enclosed in a pod which opens in two halves. It belongs to the family of crucifers, along with the cabbage and the turnip, plants characterized by four petals arranged in the shape of a cross, and by their four sepals.

Where hedges enclose meadows and crops, hawthorn and blackthorn, along with other plants, make up fences of foliage which provide a home for many animals, ranging from the little owl to insects sheltering for the winter. The hawthorn is known for the sharp thorns which cover its branches. In April or May its white flowers give out a delightful perfume. Its little red fruits, called haws, ripen in the summer.

The blackthorn grows into hedges which are impossible to climb through, because the plant has lots of sharp, woody spines. At the end of March or in April its branches are covered in white flowers which, unlike the hawthorn, come out before the leaves.

Gorse or furze is sometimes found along the edges of meadows. It flowers almost all year round, but especially in May and June.

hawthorn

blackthorn

partridge

Tropical Plantations

Farmers in tropical countries encounter the same sort of problems as farmers in temperate regions. They have a continual fight to keep the weeds down and to get rid of parasites that live on their crops, but they also have to worry about bad weather, dry conditions and torrential rain. The soil of the tropical forest floor is poor, because the rains carry away its minerals. Crops that are cultivated where tropical forests used to be, yield almost nothing after a few years.

pineapple
rice
coffee
cocoa

quelea or red-billed
dioch or weaver

Java sparrow

Some of the tropical plants are essential food crops – rice, millet, banana trees, coconut palms and date palms. Others such as sugar cane, cocoa palms and coffee shrubs give us products which we use in addition to our daily food requirements. There are also several species of plant which yield fibre for textiles and primary products for industrial use.

Of all cereal crops rice is the one which is grown over the greatest area throughout the world. This is a south-east Asian plant that was successfully introduced to Africa, America and even to Europe where it now grows in the Camargue and in Italy. It needs plenty of warmth, but it also needs to be wet. While it is growing, it is planted out into fields that are flooded with water, and before it is harvested

banana tree
coconut palm
date palm

the ground is dried out. On the plateaus of southern Asia, however, rice is grown like any other cereal and the fields are not flooded.

There are two birds which have developed a liking for rice. One of them is an African bird called the quelea or red-billed weaver bird, and the other, from southern Asia, is the Java sparrow. The quelea, found throughout all the drier parts of Africa south of the Sahara, feeds on the seeds of wild grasses for a good part of the year, but with so much cultivated land now available, it has taken to eating grains of rice and sorghum. This little perching bird is, in fact, a dreadful menace because it does so much damage. Its bell-shaped nest is woven from grasses and hung on the very end of a branch where it looks like a large fruit. The Java sparrow has also adapted to eating grain.

In India and South-East Asia, the flooded rice paddies are ideal for raising carp because they are the home of many insects, crustaceans, molluscs and worms. Water birds such as the little egret are particularly attracted to the paddies because of all the small creatures they contain. The little egret lives in Europe as well as Africa but most of the European population winters in Africa.

The coffee shrub, which originated in Ethiopia, has been taken to Central and South America, and Brazil is now the leading producer of coffee in the world. The cocoa palm, originally from tropical America (the Amazon), but also cultivated in Africa, is a small tree which has big fruits or pods. These are about 25 cm (10 in) long and contain many seeds, known as cocoa beans.

Hevea, the para rubber plant, grows naturally in the Amazon basin. It gives a white liquid or latex from which rubber is made.

Cultivated cotton bushes come from the wild varieties of Asia, Africa and America. Cotton is made from the hairs which surround the seeds.

The pineapple, originally from tropical America, is a perennial plant which flowers when it is three years old. Its juicy fruit is actually a collection of fruits on a fleshy stem protected by bracts (small accessory leaves).

The stem of sugar cane, which comes from somewhere in Indo-Malaysia, gives us a liquid from which sugar is made.

The banana, originally from South-East

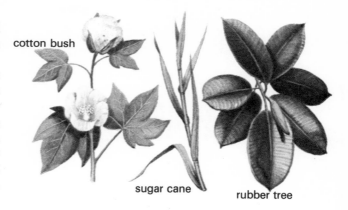

cotton bush

sugar cane   rubber tree

Asia, has been cultivated in Africa and America. It is an herbaceous plant, not a tree as one would think. The trunk is in fact formed of sheaths or envelopes of its huge leaves – they reach a size of 2.5 m by 40 cm (8 ft × 15 in) – which, piled on top of one another, make a false stem. The flower cluster measures 1 by 1.5 m (3 × 5 ft). In the wild, the flowers of the banana are pollinated by bats or birds.

The coconut palm and the date palm look like trees because of their size and their stem which is called a stipe. The stipe is like a trunk but has no branches. The diameter of the stipe is constant almost all the way up, and at the top is a plume of long leaves.

little egret

paddy fields

Index

Numbers in *italic* refer to illustrations